MODERN CHRISTIAN REVOLUTIONARIES SERIES

General Editor:

DONALD ATTWATER

I0152907

SOREN KIERKEGAARD

He who praises a man ought to follow him, and if he be not ready to follow him he ought not to praise him.—*St. John Chrysostom.*

MODERN CHRISTIAN REVOLUTIONARIES

SOREN KIERKEGAARD

A STUDY

By

MELVILLE CHANING-PEARCE

WIPF & STOCK · Eugene, Oregon

To

PAUL CHANING-PEARCE, R.A.F.V.R.

who also "ventured far out",
"visibility nil"

Wipf and Stock Publishers
199 W 8th Ave, Suite 3
Eugene, OR 97401

Soren Kierkegaard
A Study
By Chaning-Pearce, Melville
Copyright©1945 James Clarke Lutterworth Press
ISBN 13: 978-1-5326-8504-0
Publication date 3/14/2019
Previously published by James Clarke & Co., LTD., 1945

PREFACE

THIS book is not a criticism; it pretends to be no more than an exposition of Kierkegaard's main message, his revolutionary reconception of Christian truth, to our own age. I have tried therefore as far as possible to let him tell his own tale in his own terms and to add only such comments as seemed necessary to relate his word to our conditions or to show what seem to me to be the considerations necessary for a balanced criticism.

I do not pretend to that impossibility, an impartial presentation. I acknowledge Kierkegaard as my own master, and the admiration for the man and conviction of the profound importance and pertinence of his message for our own day with which I began this task have continually deepened and strengthened in the course of it. Nevertheless I have done my best to avoid special pleading and to allow Kierkegaard's words to plead for themselves.

No student of Kierkegaard can fail to realize and acknowledge his deep debt to the indefatigable labours of Dr. Walter Lowrie both as translator and as biographer of Kierkegaard, and to the Oxford University Press for making available his main works to the English-speaking world in a form so admirable and scholarly. I owe it to their courtesy that I have been able to quote so extensively from these biographies and translations, and to that of the Philosophical Society of Great Britain for the use of material in the first two chapters originally given as papers to that society, and to that of the editor of the *Hibbert Journal* for the use of an article published therein in July 1943. I also gratefully acknowledge the help given by Miss Muriel Grainger and Mrs. Sylvia Harrison.

I have done my best to simplify the knotty texture of

Kierkegaard's thought for the general reader but, if he is to speak for himself in his own often very idiomatic language, such a simplification cannot go beyond a certain point. Like all thinkers with an original thought to express Kierkegaard forged, not only his own form of faith, but also his own idiom; it is one which must be mastered before his meaning can be penetrated. It is the way of all real wisdom to conceal itself from the 'profane'; those who search for it, whether in Scripture or such commentary on Scripture as that of Kierkegaard, must be prepared to dig "in the sweat of their brow". I can only assure the reader that, if he will do so in Kierkegaard's case, he will be abundantly rewarded.

November, 1945.   M. C-P.

REFERENCES

References to the standard lives of Kierkegaard and to his own writings are shown under the following abbreviations:

L—*Kierkegaard*. By Walter Lowrie, D.D. (Oxford University Press, 1938).

L2—*A Short Life of Kierkegaard*. By Walter Lowrie, D.D. (Oxford University Press, 1943).

J—*The Journals of Soren Kierkegaard*. Edited and translated by Alexander Dru (Oxford University Press, 1938).

U.P.—*Unscientific Postscript*. By S. Kierkegaard (1838). Translated by David Swenson & Walter Lowrie (Oxford University Press, 1941).

P.F.—*Philosophical Fragments by Johannes Climacus*. Translated by David F. Swenson (Oxford University Press, 1936).

P—*From the Papers of One Still Living*. By S. Kierkegaard (1838).

S.D.—*Sickness unto Death*. By S. Kierkegaard. Translated by Walter Lowrie (Oxford University Press, 1941).

P.A.—*The Present Age*. By S. Kierkegaard. Translated by Alexander Dru and Walter Lowrie (Oxford University Press, 1940).

R.—*Repetition*. By S. Kierkegaard. Translated by Walter Lowrie (Oxford University Press, 1942).

St.—*Stages on Life's Road: Studies by Various Writers*. Collected and edited by Hilarius Bookbinder (1845).

C.D.—*Christian Discourses*. By S. Kierkegaard (1848).

P.V.—*The Point of View for My Work as an Author*. By S. Kierkegaard (1859).

T.C.—*Training in Christianity by Anti-Climacus*. Edited by S. Kierkegaard (1850).

S.E.—*For Self-Examination*. By S. Kierkegaard (1851).

CONTENTS

1

Conditions

CHRISTIANITY is both reactionary and revolutionary. It reacts to and fulfils the 'Law and the Prophets' of religious tradition; but it fulfils them with a meaning so profound or so forgotten that, in the true connotation of the term, it is also revolutionary. It revolves the orb of an eternal Wisdom, turning darkened or hitherto unrevealed aspects of it to the light. It brings out of the immemorial and inexhaustible treasure of that wisdom 'things new and old'. Its new truths are, indeed, as old as the hills; but, seen anew, they 'turn the world upside down'. Its old truths are also eternally new. Such is the basic paradox of this profoundly traditional, profoundly revolutionary faith. Because it is so, all the most profound of Christian thinkers have been both traditionalist and revolutionary, both conservative and creative.

As Dr. Lowrie has truly said, Kierkegaard "remained a conservative to the end of his days" (L. p. 91). Nevertheless, in this proper meaning of the term, there are few Christian thinkers more entitled to the style 'Christian revolutionary' than Soren Kierkegaard. The revolutionary character of his thought was also, as he constantly insisted, a reversal to the traditional truth which, so he believed, the Christianity of his time had betrayed. But, so penetrating was his insight into the treasury of Christian truth that the apostasy of Christendom which he denounced a hundred years ago to an age, in the main, incapable of understanding his meaning, is one of which our own age has become generally and ardently aware. He was, in fact, the forerunner of a Christian revolution which is only now approaching its flood-tide.

B

But – for he saw life whole and religion for him was life –
the revolution which he heralded was one not only of
religion but also of life and culture. He denounced the
whole trend of thought, both religious and secular, of the
romantic, Protestant, liberal, idealistic, pseudo-democratic
culture dominant in his day and land, and the acquisitive,
callous, comfort-loving society of *laisser-faire* individualism
which it begot in life – a way of thought and life which is
only now being seriously or generally assailed.

When to say such things seemed insane or seditious, he
declared that "Christianity does not exist" (L. p. 525), that
"parsons canonize bourgeois mediocrity" (J. 1134) and
"are trained in the art of introducing Christianity in such a
way that it signifies nothing" (P. p. 23), that "official
Christianity is both aesthetically and intellectually ludicrous
and indecent, a scandal in the Christian sense" (L2. p. 246);
he predicted a "frightful reformation" when "men will fall
away from Christianity by the millions" (L2. p. 244). In
philosophy he not only denounced the then dominant
Hegelian system of idealism but also the Cartesian logic
upon which all post-Renaissance European thought had
been built; in politics he boldly pronounced that "Christianity has nothing to do with nationalism", that "liberal
constitutions" arouse "longing for an Eastern despotism as
something more fortunate to live under" and point to "the
intensive development of the state itself" (J. 657), that "ideas
such as 'state' (*e.g.*, as it existed among the Greeks; 'Church'
in the older Catholic sense) must necessarily return" (J. 85);
in the field of culture he repudiated romanticism since it
"implies overflowing all boundaries" (J. 44), a vain vague-
ness, and found in the humanism of his age no more than
"vaporised Christianity, a culture-consciousness, the dregs of
Christianity" (J. 1209). Such criticisms are made by many
to-day and much of what he foresaw we are experiencing;
but Kierkegaard's was a voice crying almost alone in a

wilderness of nineteenth-century Protestantism, progress and complacency.

Kierkegaard's revolutionary criticism of life thus included the whole fabric of the socio-political life of the modern age in its scope, and the majority of the institutions, ideas and attitudes which he condemned are, though increasingly attacked, those with which we have still to deal to-day. And the revolution which he preached was radical; he laid his axe to the tap-root of the tree of life – the religious attitude in which such ideas and institutions originate. The present preoccupation with religion as the root of all political, economic and psychological problems echoes his prophetic diagnosis of our disease. He said that he "came out polemically against his age" (J. 588); his polemic applies no less to our own.

His constructive criticism was no less revolutionary and modern in its trend. His dialectical mode of thought anticipated the Marxian dialectic; his 'existential' thinking is a salient feature in modern philosophy and theology. His doctrine of the 'instant' and 'repetition' propounded a conception of time which is now to the fore. His insistence upon the 'leap' of life and faith as the way of reality as opposed to the 'gradualism' of the evolutionists corresponds to the most recent conclusions of biology and physics. In his call to 'inwardness' and awareness and his own profound psychological insight and fearless self-analysis he foreran modern psychology. His doctrines of the life and nature of spirit forecast that theology of the Spirit with which the religious thought of our own time is increasingly concerned.

Kierkegaard's thought is thus not only revolutionary and not limited to religion (in the cant and restricted sense of the word), it is also highly relevant to our own political, cultural and social conditions and problems. By temperament, moreover, he belonged rather to our than to his own age; he shared with the typical modern an acute sense of catastrophe and divided consciousness and, in his journals and other writings, gave to posterity a profound and searching record and analysis of that condition. The realization of the conditioned nature of all our thought and conduct is only to-day becoming general. Kierkegaard recognized the fact a century ago and, in his searching self-scrutiny and 'existential' thinking, applied that philosophically revolutionary conclusion to all the problems which confronted him. The sources of his thought are, therefore, in a degree rare among philosophers and theologians, to be traced to his own physical and psychological conditions and some knowledge of those conditions is essential for the comprehension of his work.

§

His outer history was singularly uneventful. His real drama was inward and of the spirit; it was not the less dramatic, catastrophic or tragic for that. He was born in Copenhagen in 1813. His father was a prosperous and self-made merchant and was aged 56 when Soren, the youngest of seven children, was born. His mother, cousin to his father, had been his employee and seems to have exercised little influence in the family. His home conditions were thus those of the comfortable middle-classes, his psychological climate that of an urban, industrial, respectable, bourgeois and Protestant piety.

His father, a passionate, austere, guilt-haunted and, in a puritan form, deeply religious man, dominated both by attraction and repulsion the life of his son. He was obsessed with conviction of sin and its consequent curse upon him and his family. For he had once, in his own sad and bitter boyhood, cursed God and, particularly in his second marriage with Soren's mother, was agonizedly conscious of sexual incontinence. He carried that curse and sense of sin to the grave in a tortured contrition. It was a burden which his son was to inherit and assume as his own. Soren's mother appears in the records as a somewhat wraith-like and insignificant figure, submissive, repressed and impersonal, who made little impact upon her children; the gaunt figure of the father filled the family horizon. It is not hard to reconstruct that grim and gloomy world. It is a family scene of which we have many examples in our own Victorian age; a remarkably similar situation is described in Edmund Gosse's *Father and Son.*

Soren himself, a somewhat sickly son of elderly parents and in-breeding and, as is common in such cases, hypersensitive and intellectual in bent, was acutely responsive to such oppressive conditions. The massive personality of his father imposed upon the child an adult and austere form of faith. "As a child", he has recorded, "I was strictly and austerely brought up in Christianity . . . a child crazily travestied as a melancholy old man" (L. p. 48). As he grew to manhood he fluctuated between a reverent affection for and resentment and rebellion against his father. But the latter's influence remained dominant to the end and was the mould of his piety. It was from his father that he learned how to live with God; "I have, quite literally, lived with God as one lives with one's father" (J. 771), he writes towards the end of his life. It seems certain that it was his father's costly confession to him of his own failings and faith which precipitated his own conversion and he continually testifies to the depth of his debt to him. It was undoubtedly to this dominating relationship with his father that the markedly patriarchal pattern of his piety and his insight into the mystery of the fatherly love of God are due; it seems symbolic of that relation that the only memorial of his grave is a slab which leans against his father's tomb.

Physical frailty and mental instability dogged all the seven children of this ill-balanced marriage and only two of them, the eldest and youngest sons, survived their father; it was a doom which he deemed to be a curse upon his sins. Of this frailty Soren, the youngest, had more than his share. It is probable that he suffered from spinal weakness all his life though the particular malady to which he so often alluded has never been certainly diagnosed. He was, to use his own term, an 'extraordinarius' from his school-days to his grave and his physical and psychical idiosyncrasies, combined with the unconventional clothes which he was made to wear at school, fostered a precocious brilliance at the cost of social misery. His school gave him a grounding in grammar which was to give a respect for 'the rule' and a dialectical bias to his mind, while his religious education, undertaken by his father, was a Christianity of the Cross rather than of the Resurrection, and implanted a religious melancholy which pursued him all his days. But his father seems to have given to this favoured youngest son not only his own sombre faith but also the stimulus of a teeming imagination and a powerful mind, so that Soren derived from him his aesthetic and philosophical as well as his religious bias; the double link thus forged with his father was never really broken. His favoured status as a Benjamin in the family seems also to have permitted to him a pertness to which his later love of polemics may be traced.

In 1830, at the age of 17, he proceeded from the Copenhagen high school to the university with a view to ordination—a prospect with which he flirted but never fulfilled throughout his life; he remained a student at the university for ten years. For several years he lived the life of a brilliant, wayward, dilettante, mildly self-indulgent and wild young undergraduate, and until the age of twenty-two does not seem to have desired or approached an adult attitude towards life. Until 1837 he continued to live in his father's house but his relations with him became increasingly strained. In youthful reaction from paternal domination Soren played the prodigal son, and the deepening gloom at home was aggravated by the role of elder brother which the eldest son, Peter, seems to have adopted as to the manner born.

At the university he threw himself with zest into the course of liberal studies which preceded specialization in theology, and he passed his second examination with higher honours in philosophy and science than in the classics and Hebrew. He revelled in the "up-and-down and down-and-up of thought" (L2. p. 56) for its own sake and showed an intellectual integrity which he never lost. He found passionate delight in art, particularly in music and the drama, and showed at this stage all the signs of developing into an aesthete. He gained a reputation as a wit and exercised his polemical bent at debating societies. Like most brilliant young undergraduates he posed as a *flâneur* and, in spite of a liberal allowance, accumulated debts which his father was forced to pay.

This phase of irresponsibility terminated with his twenty-second birthday in 1835, when he experienced what he has termed the 'great earthquake'. In the family circle matters had been moving during the previous few years to a climax of disaster. Before 1832 two of the seven children had already died. In the following two years Soren's brother, two sisters (including his favourite Petrea) and mother died. In the next year Soren became acquainted with his father's guilty secret – the fact, it seems probable from the evidence, that he had violated his second wife when, though a relative, in a menial capacity in the house, before he had married her. In the following spring Soren met Regina Olsen, to whom he became engaged six years later.

These events violently forced the young Kierkegaard from the childish fantasy world in which till then he had lived. But it was the disclosure of his father's guilt which most of all caused for him what he has called a "frightful upheaval" in the course of which he was "inwardly rent asunder" (L2. p. 9). For this was ruin at the very roots of his being, so rooted, as has been seen, in his father's influence. A due appreciation of this profound psychological crisis is the master-clue to the division of consciousness which scarred him to the end and to the paradoxical mode of his thinking; here too is the *fons et origo* of his otherwise incomprehensible and, for some, reprehensible, behaviour in his love-affair with Regina Olsen. In a thinly-veiled autobiographical story entitled 'Solomon's Dream' he wrote of a "rift in his nature" (L2. p. 70); it was at this time, in his twenty-second year, that this rift opened; it was a rift only to be closed by his hard-forged faith.

The immediate effect of this 'great earthquake' was to drive him to defiance, not only of his father, but also of God, and to beget in him a violent "offense at the religious" which manifested itself for several years in a bitter breach with his father, in a preference for philosophy rather than religion, and a life of increased dissipation. He was in fact in full rebellion and, as he recognized later, rebellion against his father implied rebellion against God; his infidelity at this time was a matter, not of intellect, but of will. "It is so difficult to believe", he wrote, "because it is so difficult to obey" (L2. p. 86). It was during this period that he girded at "the strange, stuffy atmosphere which we encounter in Christianity" and its "narrowbreasted asthmatic conceptions" and indulged in utopian conceptions of a "republic of science and learning" (L. p. 112). He was to some extent, plainly transferring to Christianity in general the particular stuffiness of the religion which clouded his unhappy home in such strictures, but the antipathy for this malady of conventional Christianity remained to colour his attack upon the established church at the end of his life, and the humanism which he now imbibed with such zest gave a peculiar vitality to the religion which he was later to regain.

The nadir of this phase of irreligion and rebellion came in

the year 1836 when he employed himself for his thesis on 'The Concept of Irony'; it was a theme congenial to his, at this time, somewhat mordant and inhuman wit. Alienated from faith and feeling, he lived in an egotistic world of ideas and art. "I grasped solely at the intellectual side of man's nature and clung to it . . . the idea my only joy . . . men were to me indifferent" (L2. p. 92), he wrote. But in all his diversions he was deeply divided and miserable; while his mind occupied itself with irony, his heart was held by despair, and the deep knowledge of dread which he then learned was later to be written in his book *The Concept of Dread*. He sought a pose of ironical observation of life but his would-be detachment was undermined by that dread which, with a remarkable psychological acumen, he knew to be "an attraction for what one fears". He feared the absolute sensuality which was, for him, the only alternative to absolute religion, and he fell to that fear during this year in a drunken visit to a brothel, thus incurring a guilt which at once seemed to fasten more surely upon him the parental curse, bred a humility which later helped him to become reconciled to his father, and was to constitute one of the causes for the breach of his engagement.

The shock of this sexual fall called his *hubris* and humanism to a halt and the two succeeding years were a time of regress towards reconciliation with his father and religion. For, with a profound piety, he recognized that repentance implied return "into the family, into the clan, into the race, back to God" (L2. p. 101). At this time he was, moreover, profoundly moved by his reading of the journal of a contemporary German writer, Georg Hamann; its immediate message to him was "Awake, thou that sleepest!" At this time also he fell in love with Regina Olsen.

On his twenty-fifth birthday in May 1838 he became reconciled with his father, then an old man of 82, who took this opportunity, it seems, to make a full confession of both

his failings and his faith to his son. Three months later his
father died, and Kierkegaard evidently believed that, by
overtaxing his strength by so costly a confession, he had
sacrificed himself for his son's sake. The reconciliation was
complete; the broken link between father and son was
reforged more firmly than before, and the obedience and
gratitude which Kierkegaard had latterly denied to his
father alive, he rendered doubly to him dead. He repented
himself back to his father and family; it was by the same
motion and act that he repented himself back to God, and
the refound religion which ensued was therefore the more
patriarchal in type.

   With this return to his father he also accepted, with a
deep filiality, the curse which had darkened his father's faith
and which he believed that he himself must inherit and ex-
piate. It became for him and his peculiar conditions the type
of the general guilt of mankind which each sinner shares,
and it is to this deep relationship with his father alive and
dead that his own profound sense of sin as an iron and in-
eluctable fact in life is to be ascribed. But with this sense of
sin he also inherited a knowledge no less deep of the mystery of paternal love. It was the full significance of fatherhood which his reconciliation had discovered, of the Divine
Fatherhood as of the human fatherhood which is the mortal
type of that 'great tradition'. It is in the light of this flash of
comprehension that he can say that Christian truth is true
"because my father told me so" (J. 785). He had plumbed
to a profound piety in the rich Latin sense of *pietas* and
thereby had also learned "what father-love is . . . the divine
father-love, the one unshakable thing in life, the true
Archimedian point" (L. p. 183). This conception of the full
pietas of faith and of the reciprocal love of God the Father
of men was henceforward the rock of his own religious
faith and his "new and infallible law of interpretation of
life". He explored that filial relation in religion to the end.

§

Return to religion swiftly succeeded return to his father. In May 1838 he experienced, with a profundity reminiscent of Pascal's 'heure et demie' of 'fire', the 'sudden', 'inexplicable' and 'indescribable joy' (J. 207) of re-conversion to Christianity. Although he disclaimed any mystical content for that experience, and in the light of our knowledge of his precedent condition of mind it may seem less 'inexplicable' to us than to him, there can be no doubt as to its force or its reality. Or as to its joy – a fact which, in view of the prevailing grimness of much of his gospel, should be stressed: "I rejoice over my joy, of, in, by, at, on, through, with my joy" (J. 207), he wrote with obvious sincerity and spontaneity. It is to be noted also that for him return to God also implied return to his Church; in July he went to public confession and received holy communion.·

His return to his father and faith also implied return to 'the race' and his engagement to Regina, also in May 1838, seems to have been undertaken in token of this acceptance of his conditions. The feminine element in his life had faded out with the deaths of his mother and sisters; in his intercourse with Regina he seems to have sought to fill that gap and to fulfil himself in his human life. He saw in marriage the fulfilment of both natural and spiritual life, and seems, though he failed to attain to it (as to the priesthood), never to have abandoned that belief. In later years he confessed in his journal – "had I had faith I should have remained with Regina" (J. 444). But he did not do so. "The next day", he wrote later, "I saw that I had made a mistake" and just under a year later he broke off the engagement and "to save her, to give her soul resiliency" (L. p. 226), he determined to try and make her believe that he did not love her and that the rupture was due to his own frivolity and worthlessness. He believed it to be both psychologically and

religiously wrong to pursue the marriage, and his reasons
for that 'great refusal' have a vital relevance for his later
thought.

From the sequence which has been sketched it will be
seen that Kierkegaard's engagement to Regina coincided
with a watershed period in his life, a phase of great inner
eruption of a peculiarly catastrophic kind – in the words of
St. John-of-the-Cross, "a fearful breaking up in the inner-
most parts", during which, in a profound conversion,
"turning about", of both religion and life, he was passing
from an irresponsible, dilettante and, in his own terms,
'erotic' and 'observer' attitude to a responsible, realistic and
religious attitude and from immaturity to a rapid maturing.
For her part, Regina seems to have been a girl who lived
very near to nature; her world was that of (in Kierkegaard's
phrase) the 'first immediacy', of naïve feeling and the 'erotic'.

It was a world which, with a mounting realization during
these years, Kierkegaard had come to realize that he must
renounce. His conversion had imbued him with a deep sense
of dedication and of personal mission. He knew himself
to be dedicated to an 'idea' – the Christian idea, and that
conversion had meant a radical change in attitude and mode
of life from 'immediacy' (natural spontaneity) to 'spirituality' – a way of life which he called the 'second immediacy'.
But Regina lived in a world of the 'first immediacy'. He
knew that, since that inner crisis, he had become "an eternity
too old for her". For, he quotes from Johan Georg Hamann,
"a man who lives in God therefore stands in the same relation to the 'natural' man that a waking man does . . . to a
dreamer. . . . He has been 'born again' . . . he has become an
eternity older . . . he has now become spirit . . ." He knew
that "essentially I live in a spirit-world" – a world of which
Regina knew nothing. "So then", he comments, "she would
have gone to smash" (L. p. 221). "My engagement to her",
he wrote elsewhere, "and the breaking of it is really my

relation to God, my engagement to God, if I may dare say so" (L2. p. 147).

This was part of the 'secret' which he could not tell her because she could not have understood. But there was more. He felt himself to be a 'penitent'. He had, so he believed, not only inherited but incurred his father's sin and curse. For he too had defied both his father and God. And he too, in a sudden blind sensuality, had been guilty of lustful incontinence. "Had I not been a penitent, had my *vita ante acta* not been melancholy", he wrote, "union with her would have made me happy as I had never dreamed of becoming" (L. p. 218). He was conscious too of his own dawning genius which "like a thunder-storm comes up against the wind" (J. 309) of the "pale, bloodless, hard-lived, midnight shapes" to which he must "give life and existence" (J. 345), and of, as he believed, "the curse which rests upon me . . . never to be allowed to let anyone deeply and inwardly join themselves to me" (J. 379). Therefore, for God's sake, for her's and for his own, he was driven to the conclusion that he must not marry.

However his motives and conduct may be construed, it is certain that it was no simple or easy sacrifice, and that for him it was a crucial decision for a Christianity which, in his conception, is compact of decision. "I loved her dearly", he declared with an indubitable sincerity, "she was as light as a bird, as daring as a thought" (J. 363). She was, in fact, the living symbol of all that his soul, his 'erotic' nature, most passionately desired. And again – "there is nothing so infinite as love" (J. 368); he could not forget her. To abandon her and, with her, his erotic desire, meant death; "when I left her", he wrote, "I chose death" (J. 655). And he died to more than Regina – a whole world. "Ce n'est pas Regina Olsen seulement," comments Leo Chestov, "c'est le monde entier qui s'est transformé pour Kierkegaard en une ombre, en une fantôme." Whatever judgement may be passed upon his behaviour, there can be no doubt that he acted from an overmastering sense of compulsion. "I had not the strength to abstain from marriage, I was compelled" (J. xxxviii), he confessed later.

However bitter that renunciation, it was not barren; in that sacrifice he was taught his truth and it is perhaps by that fruit of his act that it is rightly to be judged. Six years later he wrote, "I owe what is best in me to a girl; but I did not exactly learn it from her, I learnt it through her" (J. 761). The experience was crucial and formative for all his future life and thought. Here is the forge of his passionate and paradoxical faith, for a faith which could not adequately interpret that experience to him was of no avail. Here was the implacable conflict and dialectic of 'Yes' and 'No' in his actual existence from which sprang his Christian co-ordination of contraries, his 'existential thinking' and the dialectic, the poignant paradox, which he found at the heart of religious reality. And here was the knowledge of passion 'proved on his pulses' by the light of which he affirmed that "faith is a passion (though a passion which must be purified)" (J. 590). Therefore he perceived in paradox "the passion of thought" and judged that "the thinker who is devoid of paradox is like the lover who is devoid of passion – a pretty poor sort of fellow" (J. 335). Since his own faith was thus forged in this furnace of existential passion, he found no use for a religion not rooted in reality. Since the breach of his engagement to Regina was also the sealing of his 'engagement to God', religion was for him first and foremost a "love-story". "This relationship of mine to God", he wrote ten years later, "is the experience of a happy lover" (L. p. 441).

§

Kierkegaard's conflict and agony were poured out in books. Two years after his breach with Regina he began his serious career as a writer with four books, all written as 'indirect communication' to her: *Either-Or*, *Two Edifying Discourses*, *Repetition* and *Fear and Trembling*, all published in 1843. In 1846, in the *Unscientific Postscript*, he published a statement of the existential philosophy which is the foundation of his religious thought; it remains one of the most 'central' (as he himself described it) and important of his books; in it he challenges the whole system of Cartesian and Hegelian philosophy. In the same year he launched an attack, in the interests, as he conceived, of public decency, upon a disreputable periodical called *The Corsair*. But he had succeeded in representing himself to the public of Copenhagen (though not to Regina) as a worthless cynic, and had provoked a publicity and unpopularity of which *The Corsair* made capital in a series of anonymous lampoons. Kierkegaard learned what it meant to be "trampled to death by geese"; for his extreme sensitivity, as he wrote, "such a galling sort of abuse is about the most torturing experience" (L. p. 358).

His work and his experience up to this point had been *prolegomena* to his religious writings and, as he said, his "education in becoming a Christian" (L2. p. 186). He was then 34 years old, an age beyond which he had never expected to live. For the remainder of his life, nine years, he devoted himself to religious writing, at first under a variety of pseudonyms and later, after his second conversion in 1848, under his own name. In 1847 the first of this series, *Edifying Discourses*, appeared. In 1848 he underwent a second crisis of spirit when, as he said, "God had run me to a standstill" (L2. p. 201), of which he wrote – "My whole nature is changed . . . I must speak" (J. 747). This second crisis seems to have convinced him of his own integration as a spirit-person and of an urgent call to action. "From now on", he said, "I shall have to take over clearly and directly everything which up till now has been indirect and come forward personally, definitely and directly as one who wished to serve the cause of Christianity" (J. 806). And from now on the note of his writing is, as was said of John Donne, that of a "dying man to dying men".

This final phase is heroic. He was, in his own words, "venturing far out". He was venturing "the burden of being and becoming spirit", into what he believed to be that new dimension of spirit-being to which the Christian is called, venturing beyond his limits and daring deeds beyond his competence or his desire "by virtue of the absurd . . . trusting in God". He was venturing beyond "the erotic", beyond the plane of the sensuous poetry in which his poetic spirit had found its delight. Such poetry of earth had now for him come to seem "wishful, infatuating, benumbing"; in comparison with that, he writes, "Christianity . . . is prose . . . and yet is precisely the poetry of eternity"; like St. Paul, he declares that now "I will sing with the spirit". He was venturing what he believed would mean martyrdom in the belief that "Denmark has need of a dead man"; in fact his venturing probably precipitated his death. He was venturing an unconditional Christianity for himself and an uncompromising attack upon the conditional Christianity of the established church, "putting a match to established Christendom". Finally, he was venturing his personal security, for he was now nearly at the end of his resources; his diminishing capital ended with his life. He did so deliberately, eschewing the security of a living in the church, of the financial prudence of which he was well aware for, he wrote, "as soon as I make my life finitely secure . . . I am finitized." He was now staking all and more than he had or was upon his faith. "I have the honour", he told King Christian, "to serve a higher power, for the sake of which I have staked my life". It is not possible to study the man and his records with care without realizing that these were no heroics; he lived out his 'troubled truth'.

The immediate fruit of this new crisis and decision is to be found in his two major religious books, *Sickness unto Death* (1849) and *Training in Christianity* (1850), and in a religious biography entitled *The Point of View* (1848); his impulse to definitive and provocative action produced a frontal attack upon the established church in *The Instant* in 1855, the year of his death at the age of 42.

His Christian thinking had grown continually more challenging and unconditional; his action as a Christian in this final phase fulfilled his thought in deeds. At the end he was able to declare, in a saying reminiscent of St. Paul's apologia for his life, " . . . I have not let go of my thought, I have not made my life comfortable" (L2. p. 226). On his death-bed he refused the ministrations of the official church since he said that "the parsons are royal functionaries, and royal functionaries are not related to Christianity" (L2. p. 254). He died in the assurance of grace and joy and with, in the words of a spectator, "a sublime and blessed splendour" of appearance.

The chief characters in this intense inner drama are few in number. Kierkegaard's retiring and introverted disposition and semi-recluse existence did not conduce to the making of intimate friendships, and Emil Boesen, friend of his youth and attendant at his death-bed, seems to have been the only person to whom, apart from his family and Regina, he gave his confidence. In his later years one Rasmus Nielsen, a professor, attached himself in the role of a follower but it was a relationship which irked the unwilling rabbi. The two public contemporaries of mark for whom he had an affectionate respect, Bishop Mynster, primate of the Church of Denmark and his father's close friend and director, and Professor Martersen, popularizer of Hegel in Denmark, became, with an irony peculiarly his own, the targets of his attack upon the established order in religion and philosophy. But, although he made few friends and

c

many enemies, in his habitual saunterings in the Copenhagen streets and long carriage drives, he made acquaintance with nature and with all sorts and conditions of men
and women – a racy actuality of which he made rich use in
his writing.

In the making of his mind books played a more important
part than persons. Apart from the Bible, the dialogues of
Socrates (from whom his dialectic is largely derived), the
works of Hegel and the Jena romantics such as Fichte,
Novalis, Schelling and the Schlegels (mainly in strong
reaction), the plays of Shakespeare (in particular *Richard II,
Hamlet* and *King Lear*, which seemed to speak most poignantly to his condition) and the writings of Johan Georg
Hamann (whose conversion and attitude towards Christianity so nearly resembled his own) were the main formative influences upon his thought. Though he repudiated the
name of 'mystic' and held that "mysticism has not the
patience to wait for God's revelation" (J. 321), he studied
Gorres' *Mystik* and was acquainted with mystical writers
such as Boehme, Tauler and the Victorines.

§

The sources of Kierkegaard's profound and persistent
sense of crisis and catastrophe are to be sought chiefly in his
own inner life. But the course of public affairs in Denmark
during his lifetime fomented that feeling. He had long and
with the persistence of a Jeremiah prophesied political disaster; with the Danish-German war of 1848, as a result of
which Denmark lost Schleswig-Holstein and suffered a
constitutional revolution, the storm broke with a sense of
catastrophe for his countrymen and contemporaries which
it is not easy for an age attuned to disaster upon a scale so
much more vast to appreciate. Nevertheless Kierkegaard's
generation in Denmark lived with thunder in the air, and

his thought was shaped under the shadow of a catastrophe clearly foreseen by him. Moreover, with a prophetic vision alone sufficient to acclaim his genius, Kierkegaard foresaw what he described as the "total bankruptcy towards which the whole of Europe seems to be heading" (L. p. 157) – a bankruptcy of which our world is all too well aware. With an uncanny prescience he foresaw and foretold the whirlwind which we are reaping. He conceived it to be his duty and destiny to sound a 'cry of alarm'. It is rather as a 'corrective' (the title with which he himself described his role as he saw it) and 'cry of alarm' than as systematic theology or philosophy that his work is, with justice, to be judged.

Kierkegaard's conditions were thus evidently of a kind to render them a happy hunting-ground for psychologists. An Oedipus-complex, a father-fixation, making him at once the psychological murderer and 'spiritual wife' of his father, bi-sexuality, homosexuality, schizophrenia, paranoia are eagerly diagnosed by Freudian fanatics. It seems characteristic of his ironic humour that he should have himself anticipated them all, for he analysed himself throughout his life with a pitiless persistence and acumen unparalleled in literature. A full and modern estimate of his thought cannot indeed omit such a mode of enquiry and it is amply evident that his genius (like all genius) bordered upon the pathological.

But such enquiry serves rather to magnify than to minimize the quality of the man, for it illuminates from one angle the extreme tension to which he, like all men who, in Dr. Reinhold Niebuhr's words, stand "at the junction of nature and spirit", inherit "as the sparks fly upward". Save for a bigoted and uncritical psychological dogmatism, they cannot pass any final verdict upon the "unmapped, unmeasured, secret heart" of Kierkegaard or any other genius. Nor can they, as is sometimes so glibly assumed, denigrate the spark of spirit, the flame of personal truth born in the womb of genius from such inner conflict. In the words of Henri Massis (Les Idées Restent, p. vii) "là où l'èsprit est libre, actif, il n'y a pas de désastre irreparable" for a soul, such as that of Soren Kierkegaard, wrestling, 'free' and 'active' to the end, with its psychological contraries.

Such psychological criticism, however, serves to emphasize the kinship of Kierkegaard's spirit with the temper, so conscious of a similar division of consciousness, of our own age. It is thus with a special sense of affinity that the more aware of modern men can contemplate the inner drama of Kierkegaard's life and the knotty texture of his thought. For, with a lonely heroism of spirit which can but elicit the admiration of the understanding, he confronted, a century before its full time, a conflict of consciousness of which the majority of Europeans have only recently become aware. But it is with the wisdom born from that travail of soul and seen in the perspective of our knowledge of his conditions that we are concerned. In such a presence preconceived formulas and dogmas are best laid by.

2

Existential Thinking

THE foundations of Kierkegaard's faith were laid in his own life; the only truth which was of any value for him was that which was 'existential', which spoke to his own suffering and corresponded with the paradox, conflict and despair so poignantly experienced in his own individual existence and passion. He had known the paradox and dialectic of life and love, the extremity of inner division and had plumbed the depths of human futility. "I stick my finger into existence – it smells of nothing", he wrote in *Repetition*. It was in this 'tension of reality' that his thought was rooted and for such a 'sickness unto death' in his own experience of human existence that he sought a 'radical cure' in an 'existential truth'. Both his need and his psychological state were thus remarkably similar to those of our own time.

Such a personal truth had always been his aim. When only 22 he had already stated his life's quest. "The thing is to understand myself, to see what God really wished *me* to do; the thing is to find *the idea for which I can live and die*" (the italics are Kierkegaard's). That truth was alone true for him which he could, in Keats's phrase, "prove upon his pulses". Such a truth he styled 'existential'. It is a term which is fundamental for his faith and now in common use – and abuse. It therefore requires careful consideration.

Although modern 'existential philosophy' largely derives from the thought of Kierkegaard, he himself never precisely defined the term. But he has stated what 'existence' implied for him. "Existence is the child of the infinite and the finite, the eternal and the temporal, and is therefore constantly striving . . . an existing individual is constantly in process of

becoming" (U.P. p. 79). Existence thus implies for Kierkegaard not the calm of being but the conflict of becoming,
and not life in the abstract, but conditioned human life lived
in the 'tension of reality'. The 'existing individual' exists
on the frontier between time and eternity, finite and
infinite, a –

> "... swinging-wicket set
> Between
> The Unseen and the Seen."

He is, in Dr. Reinhold Niebuhr's words, "under the tension
of finiteness and freedom, of the limited and the unlimited".
It is to this specifically human predicament in existence that
Kierkegaard's use of the word refers, with such existence
that his 'existential thought' is concerned and by such
existence that he believes it to be conditioned. He thus
anticipated the notion of the conditioned nature of all
thought and of the 'tension of faith' upon which such
leaders of modern thought as Professor Karl Mannheim and
Dr. Niebuhr to-day insist.

It is thus with such actual existence that, for Kierkegaard,
real thinking is alone concerned, and by its conditions that it
is itself conditioned. Thinking which recognizes such existence as at once its only real subject-matter and its test of
truth and that the thinker is himself, as an 'existing individual', immersed in the conditions of his existence and
therefore "in process of becoming", is for him 'existential
thinking' – the thought of "the whole man facing the whole
mystery of life". In Dr. Paul Tillich's definition of this type
of thought, "truth is bound to the existence of the knower
... Only so much of knowledge is possible as the degree to
which the contradictions of existence are recognized and
overcome" (*The Interpretation of History*, p. 63).

But it is important to observe that, for Kierkegaard, experience of existence is not limited to the experience of

personal human existence apart from God; it includes the existence of God. For God has himself entered into existence and the existential experience of man; "the God-Man is himself the existential" (J. 1054). Of his existence Kierkegaard is as sure as of his own with the steadfast conviction of Browning's " . . . thy soul and God stand sure".

That initial faith in the existence of God in human history and in his own individual experience is, for Kierkegaard, his datum; he accepts it as axiomatic and beyond either proof or dispute; it is, not rational, but faith-knowledge. That some such premise which is always in reality, not rational, but faith-knowledge lies at the root of all thought is obvious; the rationalist could not reason unless he believed in the validity of reason and this he cannot know, he can only believe. For Kierkegaard this dual premise of the existence of his own soul and God was his 'jumping-off point'. He believed that both existences are knowable by the individual's inner experience of existence and are, indeed, only by such an 'inwardness' to be known at all. And it is this, to reason, apparent contradiction and 'absurdity' of the entry of being into becoming, essence into existence, God into history, which constitutes the tension and paradox of life and necessitates a dialectical mode of thinking – a simultaneous Yes and No.

Therefore the datum of existential thinking and the existential test of truth are, for Kierkegaard, dual—the existence and experience of, not only self, but God. It is this supremely important fact which differentiates the 'existentialism' of Kierkegaard from that of the nazis. The latter accept and affirm the existence of man (in the abstract) only; Kierkegaard accepts and affirms the existence of both man and God. Therefore the criticism of existential philosophy delivered by Miss Dorothy Emmet in *Philosophy* (July 1941) that it implies "no external standard of truth and

morality above the individual decision", while true of the
nazi form of existentialism, is false for that of Kierkegaard.
For he, in his experience of existence, posits both the subjective standard of self-knowledge and the objective
standard of knowledge of God. For him the nazi form of
existentialism is unexistential since it omits the greater part
of existential experience.

The test of truth for Kierkegaard and all existential
Christian thinking which accepts his dual premise is thus an
existential decision or apprehension of the self when confronted with the objective reality of life and God. It is not
some arbitrary and arrogant 'private judgement' of the self
upon life and God, and as such subject to the manifold
corruption and fallibility of all human judgement. It is that
truth and conviction which are struck from the meeting
of the subjective and inward 'passion' or feeling of the
'whole man' with a reality and revelation which, though
apprehended subjectively, are, in fact, utterly objective to
him.

It is, indeed, like his own apprehension, embodied in and
conveyed to him by tradition. For tradition (that which is
handed across the generations to the individual) both conditions the 'passion' of the individual and confronts him in
the Great Tradition of history and revelation. Thus the
tradition of Christian truth is conveyed to him by the
Christian Church. It is to this objective element in existential truth that Kierkegaard refers when he says that he
accepts Christian truth "because my father told me so".
Thus an existential decision after the pattern of Kierkegaard
in fact includes "an external standard of truth and morality"
as a major factor in its decision. The ultimate decision is
itself dialectical; from the opposition and meeting of the
individual soul and God a new condition, that of faith, is
born. To pose the process in simple Christian language, the
soul, when confronted by Christ, is constrained to obey that

call of reality; when it does so it becomes a 'new man' and leads a 'new life'.

Existential thinking is thus based upon a primary postulate which is the precise contrary of that of Descartes from which the whole of the Cartesian and idealistic philosophy, liberal sociology, scientific evolutionism and humanism of the modern age derive. Where Descartes declared that "I think, therefore I am", Kierkegaard retorted, "I am, therefore I think". For the one, abstract thought, for the other, concrete and total existence was the foundation of faith. Both thus accept primary postulates which cannot be proved. The Cartesian and humanist accept their fundamental faith in the validity and sovereignty of the human reason upon the supposed evidence of human experience; Kierkegaard accepts his faith in the existence of himself and God upon the evidence of an existential experience which includes both human feeling and divine revelation. His revolution in thought was thus of the most radical kind which can be conceived and one which, if accepted, must reorientate the whole course of thought and life.

This fundamental faith not only provides the ultimate criterion of truth; it also shapes to its pattern all thought and life proceeding from it. For Descartes and his followers truth is that which is true for thought; for Kierkegaard and existential thinkers it is that which is true for life. For the former, intellect, for the latter, the whole personality in its 'human predicament' is dominant and decisive. The one necessarily tends towards a predominantly rational and intellectual, the other towards a vital and intuitive way of life and thought.

The revolt against the Cartesian philosophy and that which ensued from it and dominated European thought in Kierkegaard's day is now general. It has recently been well expressed by Mr. H. J. Massingham. "What he [Descartes] did", he writes, "was to elevate man above his proper station, above, that is to say, his 'creatureliness' by his intellectual gospel of egocentricity. 'I am', he wrote, 'because I think'. Neither God nor 'I' were realities, both being intellectual abstractions" (*The Tree of Life*, p. 109). But in Kierkegaard's day such a denunciation of the dominant dogma of philosophy was a radical revolution in the realm of ideas. It is a revolution which is still in process to-day.

This revolutionary doctrine of the nature of human truth and human thinking gives to 'existential thinking' characteristics which were quite contrary to those of the prevalent idealistic philosophy. In the first place, it is a different mode of thought and therefore begets a different type of thinker. While the tradition of Descartes produced philosophers and scientists who seek to be detached observers of life, 'above the battle', that of Kierkegaard produced thinkers involved in the concrete battle of existence, and it is noteworthy that Kierkegaard repudiated the title of 'philosopher' and preferred that of a 'Christian thinker'.

As Professor Karl Heim has said of Kierkegaard's type of thought, "a proposition or truth is said to be *existential* when I cannot apprehend or assent to it from the standpoint of a mere spectator but only on the ground of my total existence" (*God Transcendent*, p. 75). Such thinkers are 'educated by experience' rather than by thought. Since their "concern implies relationship to life, to the reality of personal existence", they therefore renounce both "the high aloofness of indifferent learning" and "scientific aloofness from life". And since they are primarily concerned, not with thinking, but with living, their thinking is, to employ a phrase now popular in scientific circles, 'operational'; it is "drawn from life and expressed again in life" (L. p. 214).

Therefore Kierkegaard and 'existential thinking' repudiate all abstract thinking and thinkers. Thus he asserts that "the sciences . . . reduce everything to calm and objective observation" and, therefore, that "the whole of science is a parenthesis". Again he denounces "the hopeless forest fire of abstraction" and is acid in his comments upon 'dons' and 'professors'. The don is "a man in whom there is nothing human, where enthusiasm and the desire to act . . . is concerned, but who believes it to be a learned question". 'The truth' is crucified like a thief, mocked and spat upon – and dying, calls out, "Follow me". Only the 'don' (the inhuman being) understands not a single word of it all, he construes it all as a learned problem. One is to suffer; the other is to become a professor of the fact that another has suffered" (J. 1362). "Take away the paradox from the thinker and you have the professor" (L. p. 506) 'Parsons' come under the same condemnation but, in so far as they are 'observers' of the passion of God their offence is the more rank.

Second, existential thinking proposes a different objective to that of abstract philosophy and science; it is concerned, not with intellectual proofs or certainty, but with pragmatic faith; "certainty can only be had in the infinite, where he (the existing subject) cannot remain, but only repeatedly arrives" (U.P. p. 75). For Kierkegaard this "prolix knowledge . . . this certainty which lies at faith's door and lusts after it" is anathema. Therefore abstract philosophy unrelated to life (as he conceived the Hegelian system to be) is both futile and fatal for faith, which alone matters. For while "a logical system is possible, a system of existence is impossible" (L. p. 308). "Existence must be content with a fighting certainty". The quest for certainty, which is the quest of such a philosophy, has thus nothing whatever to do with existential truth, or with Christianity as Kierkegaard conceives it, "wherein", he writes, "lies the misunderstanding between speculation and Christianity" (L. p. 301). Therefore, for him, "Christianity and philosophy cannot be reconciled" (J. 32).

Third, since existential thinking is concerned with "the reality of personal existence", it is not objective but subjective, not coldly external to life but inward with an "endless passion" of "inwardness", not impersonal, but profoundly personal. "The real task is to be objective to oneself and subjective towards all others". (J. 676)

But by 'subjectivity' Kierkegaard does not mean mere individualism or that the individual judgement is the measure of all things. The term is used by him in opposition to the Hegelian claim to objectivity or personal disinterestedness in the effects of speculative thinking. The subjective thinker, for Kierkegaard, is not he who judges solely by subjective standards and private judgement but he who is concerned with the truth for him and his own concrete situation. Moreover by subjectivity he also implies personality, a spiritual person derived from and dependent upon a transcendent God known to him in his own 'inwardness'.

This emphasis upon the personal apprehension of truth is perhaps Kierkegaard's most important contribution to modern thought; it is one which gives him a spiritual paternity to that 'personalism' which, with Berdyaev, Maritain and many more, is now in the van of philosophical and political speculation. In Professor Theodor Haecker's judgement "the being and essence of the person are the elements which Kierkegaard brought into philosophy" (*Soren Kierkegaard*, p. 29).

Fourth, existential thinking is not dispassionate (as philosophy aspires to be) but passionate. "Passion is the real thing, the real measure of man's powers. And the age in which we live is wretched, because it is without passion" (J. 396). For him both truth and faith are passions. But he equates passion with *pathos*, in its proper Greek sense of feeling or suffering – a suffering to which mind and soul as well as body are subject. He is careful to discriminate it, in this sense, from what he calls "unshaven passion" and insists that "passion must be purified".

He emphasizes the fact that "passion and feeling are open to all men in an equal degree"; here is the basis of the universalism which he constantly and vehemently affirms. Such an exaltation of 'passion' or feeling as a primary means for the apprehension of truth is therefore profoundly democratic in tendency. For, since all can feel but few can reason in the meaning of rationalism, truth is thus within the reach, not merely of a learned *élite*, but of every man who has been schooled by suffering.

This conception of 'passionate' thinking is also closely akin to the mystic approach to reality, though Kierkegaard repudiated the pseudo-mysticism which, as he wrote, "has not the patience to wait for God's revelation" (J. 321). Thus "by love may he be gotten and holden; but by thought never" it is written in the *Cloud of Unknowing*, where a form of knowledge is expounded " . . . not coming from without . . . by the windows of the wits, but from within". Such a *via mystica* is evidently of the same order as the Kierkegaardian way of 'passion' and 'inwardness'.

It seems clear, indeed that he ranks 'passion' or feeling higher than abstract reason in the scale of apprehension of existential truth. Upon the premise that it is "the whole man facing the whole mystery of life" who can alone reach reality, it must be so. For, while such reason is rare and at one remove from reality, feeling is universal and immediate.

In so far as it denies to abstract reason and intellect the monopoly of truth, existential thinking thus tends towards anti-intellectualism and even irrationalism. For Kierkegaard "the intelligence and all that goes with it has done away with Christianity . . . the fight is against intelligence" (J. 925). In the modern tendency towards irrationalism and the popular feeling against 'intellectuals' and 'highbrows'

Kierkegaard's revolt against the tyranny of rationalism is peculiarly modern in its trend. But the tendency towards irrationalism in such 'corrective' sayings has been exaggerated by some of his successors. Thus a modern disciple of Kierkegaard, Miguel de Unanumo, declared that "reason is the enemy of life. A terrible thing is intelligence . . . All that is vital is irrational" (*The Tragic Sense of Life*, pp. 90–1).

It seems very doubtful whether Kierkegaard would have endorsed such statements. Intellect, abstract reason and analytical science are for him not primary, but they are secondary; they are servants of the human spirit which have usurped the sovereign seat of the existential decision of the 'whole man' and, as such, are to be fought. But he nowhere suggests that reason is not an important element in the apprehension of the whole man to which he appeals, and he himself attacks what he believes to be a false use of reason with the weapons of reason. Indeed he specifically declares that "the race must go through reason to the absolute" (J. 1256). But "Life can only be explained after it has been lived" (J. 192), he wrote, and he himself devoted his life to explaining it. He does not deny the need to explain life; he is concerned to put rational explanation in its proper place in the approach of man to reality.

Moreover, the reason which Kierkegaard attacked was neither reason in the Greek sense of *nous* nor that 'natural reason' to which, according to St. Thomas Aquinas, "all are compelled to assent"; on the contrary the 'existential thinking' which he desired had much in common with these conceptions of reason, as also with the 'understanding' of the "Wisdom literature" of the Old Testament. It was the cold, abstract, analytic and arrogant reason of the Cartesian school which Hegel, as he thought, had inherited, which he condemned.

Fifth, the whole man, by virtue of such 'passion' in existential thinking, is believed to be capable, in Dr. W. M.

Horton's words, of "consciousness of an extra dimension of reality inaccessible to the cool intellect but accessible to a warmer and more vital faculty" (*Contemporary Continental Theology*, p. 90); existential thinking opens the door to new realms of reality and 'faith-knowledge' of which 'intellect' can know nothing. "With the eyes of the heart I read it", Kierkegaard declares. It is a mode of comprehension of which Pascal wrote, "le cœur a ses raisons que la raison ne connaît point" – the heart has its reason which reason knows not. For with that 'eye of the heart', so the existentialist claims, the "world of reality" which is "the world of qualities" (not of quantities) can be perceived. By such an existential approach, in Rilke's phrase, "the heart is born into the whole".

Sixth, since man's existential apprehension of reality is that of his 'human predicament', a state of constant and, in time, irresolvable tension between 'mighty opposites'; that tension and conflict can no more be eliminated from real thinking than from real life. He is everywhere inescapably conscious of contradiction and paradox in his existential experience; it is the paradox, the clash of contraries in life which causes its passion. Therefore, for existential thinking, paradox must also be "the passion of thought" and " . . . the thinker who is devoid of paradox is like the lover who is devoid of passion – a pretty poor sort of fellow". "Take away the paradox from the thinker and you have the professor". "The paradox", Kierkegaard writes, "is really the *pathos* of the intellectual life". It is "a category of its own", with its own dialectic.

The predominance of paradox in existential thinking and in the thought of Kierkegaard is thus, in his use of it, no wilful or obscurantist irrationalism but (since it is the very texture of the 'tension of life') also the very texture of the only real reasoning which the human mind, thus conditioned by tension and paradox, can achieve. All reasoning which seeks to smooth out that paradox is therefore both unrealistic and arrogant.

Seventh, since the speech of paradox is dialectic and "existence is surely a debate", the dialectic of paradox is the proper mode of existential thought. This dialectical mode of thought has been lucidly described by Canon V. A. Demant: "Dialectical thinking . . . bids us look for the unity behind any pair of conflicting opposites and leads us to expect a re-emergence of something which will stand in relation to the original unity of both as the same and not the same, like it but on a new plane" (*Christian Polity*, pp. 152–3). It is thus "the opposite of continuity thinking which conceived change as the sum of increments of movements in one direction".

For Kierkegaard the necessity for such dialectical thinking is proved by his existential apprehension, through passion or feeling, of the double paradox of his own experience and the Incarnation, the two axiomatic facts from which all his thinking derives. Of the paradox of his own experience he has written in *Repetition* and his journals; for Christianity "the eternal truth has to come into time, this is the Paradox" (L. p. 319). Yet "if man is to receive any knowledge about the Unknown [God] he must be made to know that it is unlike him, absolutely unlike him" (P.F. pp. 36–7). "As a sinner man is separated from God by a yawning qualitative abyss" (S.D. p. 199).

Therefore, again to quote Dr. Horton, "a truly reverent theology, which knows that God is in heaven and man on earth, must never pass directly from human thought and experience to God, as Schleiermacher and Hegel sought to do. It must reverse the Hegelian dialectic . . . look for no synthesis on the earthly plane, but balance every thesis with an antithesis, every Yes with a No, and then, standing helplessly in the contradiction, appeal to God for a revelation, and act of grace" (*op. cit*, p. 101). The dialectic of paradox thus leads direct to a doctrine of despair – despair of all attempts of the intellect or any other human faculty fully to comprehend the paradox either of man's own existence or that of God.

Existential thinking thus leads to an abyss which thought cannot cross; Kierkegaard's conclusion is that of Jan van Ruysbroek: "we must all found our lives upon a fathomless abyss" – an abyss which can only be crossed by the 'leap in the dark' which is faith, that "happy passion". But, for existential thinking, faith itself remains a 'tension'. Existential truth is thus a 'troubled truth' which points to despair and so to the decision of faith.

In the meaning of Kierkegaard 'existential thinking' is thus a mode of thought which accepts the tension of life and is therefore concrete not abstract, subjective and personal not objective and impersonal, passionate (in the sense of suffering) not dispassionate, which seeks, not rational proof for thought but the assurance of faith for life and claims to explore a dimension of reality closed to the analytical reason, which carries the paradox of life into the process of living thought and employs in that thought a dialectic which the recognition of that paradox requires, which expects its synthesis, not in time and the mind of man, but in eternity and the mind of God.

It is a mode of thought which begins, as has been seen, with a religious affirmation of the existence of the self and of God, and ends with a declaration of despair and points to the 'leap' of faith as the only 'radical cure' of that despair. It is conditioned and 'operational' thinking of a kind which completely reverses the 'continuity' systems of Cartesian, idealistic and evolutionary philosophy and science. Its fundamental proposition is that "truth is bound to the situation of the knower".

It is thus, in all respects, a mode of thought which is remarkably modern and apposite to our age. It is also one

D

which, as Dr. Tillich has pointed out, speaks the same language of thought (though not of faith) as Marxian Communism. For such a truth, "bound to the individual situation in Kierkegaard", is of the same order as the Marxian dialectic which is bound "to the social situation in Marx" (*op. cit.*, p. 63). In the case of Kierkegaard, owing to his initial and axiomatic faith not only in the existence of self but also in that of the God-man, it inevitably leads to a Christian faith reconsidered by such an 'existential thinking'. That faith remains to be explored.

3

The Foundations of Faith

KIERKEGAARD's criticism of contemporary Christianity and his reconception of what he believed to be a real Christianity are based upon his principle of existential thinking. It led him to a profound religious realism which could only reject much of the religion of his time as unreal, and to what may be termed an existential Christianity of the spirit.

Whatever our estimate of his criticisms and conclusions, it is difficult at this distance, adequately to estimate the lonely courage or the cost of that enterprise, or to reckon its full impact upon our life, thought and faith. It was a revolution, not only in the realm of ideas but also of faith, far more radical than that which begot the French Revolution; it is one which seems only now to be approaching its high tide in the thought and faith of the Western world.

In its heyday Kierkegaard assailed the then undisputed sovereignty of the abstract, analytical, systematizing reason which, since the Renaissance and Descartes, had increasingly dominated European thought and life. He substituted for it an existential apprehension, not by detached and isolated intellect alone, but by the whole human person in, from and for his existing conditions. He sought a living truth for life rather than an ideal but dead truth for thought, and applied the logic of that principle uncompromisingly to Christian thinking. The task involved the reconsideration from this existential angle of the whole Christian tradition which he had inherited.

It was an inevitable stage in his own progress towards spiritual maturity and literally a matter of life and death for him. He was forced by his own existential need to find a truth by which he could live and die. As for Hamlet (with whom, in the crucial and formative phase of his thought, he felt so strong an affinity), the double discovery of the guilt of his father and the impossibility of marriage with the woman he loved had destroyed his natural zest for life and will to live – what he termed his 'first immediacy'. He had been driven inwards by his fate to the dark foundations of his being and to Hamlet's ultimate agony of "to be or not to be". He had come to the abyss at which pure thought ends and to the knowledge that "suicide is the only tolerable existential consequence of pure thought" (U.P. p. 273). He must find the "second immediacy" of the "new man" or cease to be.

No light humanism or hedonism could for long suffice a mind so powerful, profound and acute, a nature so passionate or an integrity so exacting. His early training in Christianity, his father's influence and the force of his own conversion in 1838 had rooted within him a fundamental faith in God and the Christian vision of life which no storm could destroy. His soul, like that of the modern Western world, was too deeply christianized to permit of any pre- or sub-Christian faith. He might rebel against the form of Christianity which he encountered; he might flirt with infidelity as a gesture of defiance, but he could not really escape from the Christian pattern of life and thought. His problem was not that of proving Christian truth, but of reconciling that truth with the reality which he knew, of finding a reconception of Christianity for which "the very being of truth is life, as the truth was in Christ" (T.C. p. 201). He must reconcile Christianity with the catastrophe which had come upon him or perish. It is a pass to which many come to-day.

To do so he was forced to a ruthless search of the foundations of his thought, his faith and himself. That search led him, by way of a profound self-analysis which remarkably anticipates modern psychology, to a radical reconception of Christianity as essentially a religion of inwardness and the spirit. But much demolition had to be done before that faith could be so reconceived and recaptured.

It was, by constraint of his own inner necessity, a faith built upon foundations of dread, despair and suffering to which (like our own age) he had been driven; his regress to religion was, in his own words, "a stern education from innate dread to faith" (L. p. 129). By temperament he was peculiarly susceptible to dread. At the age of twenty-six he had written, "the whole of existence frightens me, from the smallest fly to the mystery of the Incarnation" (J. 72). He analysed it as "a desire for what one fears . . . an alien power which takes hold of the individual" (J. 105). That dread included Christianity: "I felt a dread of Christianity and yet felt myself strongly drawn to it" (J. 321). He wrote in 'Nebuchadnezzar', evidently out of his own experience, "my thoughts terrified me, the thoughts in my mind, for my mouth was closed, and none could hear aught but a cry like that of a beast" (J. 567).

For him there lay, upon one side of that dread, despair or utter sensuality, on the other, Christianity; each was an abyss dark with dread. "There is only one proof of the truth of Christianity", he wrote, "and that, quite rightly, is from the emotions, when the dread of sin and a heavy conscience torture a man into crossing the narrow line between despair bordering upon madness and Christianity. *There* lies Christianity" (J. 926). There, in any case, lay Christianity for Kierkegaard.

This emphasis upon suffering was no mere masochism. Of that danger he was well aware. He knew his own abnormal capacity for suffering but remained convinced that the cost of the deeper insight into the Christian mystery which could alone suffice his need was a suffering proportionately more intense. He believed too that some were elected to such a martyrdom for the benefit of mankind. "In every generation", he wrote, "there are two or three who are sacrificed for the others, are led by frightful sufferings to discover what redounds to the good of others. So it was in my melancholy I understood myself as singled out for such a fate" (P.V. p. 79). Nor did he conceive such suffering to be only the pre-condition of Christianity; he perceived that it exacted a constant and an accumulating suffering. "This is the test: to become and remain a Christian through sufferings with which no other human sufferings can compare" (T.C. p. 194).

This stress upon suffering is evidently attributable in some degree, first, to his own abnormal sensitivity and, second, to his violent reaction from the cushioned and complacent Christianity which, in his own crisis, had been found wanting. A synthetic view of the whole of his writings suggests that, to some extent, he was deliberately stressing this feature of Christianity as a 'corrective'. He was not attempting to see Christianity whole; his existential approach precluded such a purpose. He was passionately seeking a Christianity true for him and his own problems and conditions. And he was of the 'twice-born' type. It seems therefore rather as a corrective and a particular approach than as a comprehensive *summa* of the Christian faith that his "troubled truth" is to be estimated. His word is essentially prophetic: he is rather the mountain or desert guide than the settler or cultivator of the Christian inheritance. He climbs Pisgah; he does not cultivate Canaan. The religious dialectic of twice- and once-born, prophet and priest, is one surmounted only by the saints, and in this respect also Kierkegaard was a dialectician. It is precisely because he is so that he can speak so cogently to the suffering and despair of our own age.

In his stress upon the suffering which Christianity entails he counted the cost before making the venture of faith. For he conceived that venture as an act of deliberate choice: "the decisive mark of Christian suffering is that it is voluntary" (T.C. p. 111). Despair itself is an act of decision – a voluntary awareness of self and of the real and dire issues with which the Christian challenge confronts the conscious self; "choose then despair, for despair itself is a choice." And the choice of despair is also the choice of self: "when anyone chooses despair he chooses again . . . He chooses his own self." He thus chooses both 'the absolute' and himself in his 'eternal worth'. It is a double choice – the choice, not only of conscious selfhood, but also of the reality, the not-self which confronts self. In that choice and the self born from it, freedom is also born: "the individual by persisting in his despair at last wins himself," and with self, the freedom of the spirit.

But that crucial choice in which the individual and the Christian are born is also the choice of death – the death of the pseudo-self of natural life: "death comes first, you must first die to every earthly hope, every merely human reliance, you must die to your selfishness, or to the world" (L. p. 475). The life beyond that death is the life of faith, the reborn spirit-self and eternal life. "Faith, this gift of the Holy Spirit, only appears when death has come between . . . Faith is against understanding, faith is on the other side of death . . . when it is dark as the dark night . . . then comes the life-giving Spirit and brings faith" (L. p. 477).

This death from which faith and spirit are born is the death of the 'first immediacy' that the 'second immediacy' of eternal life may come to be; its anguish is the "suffering which is involved in the dying away from immediacy." This 'self-annihilation' implied the denial of the aesthetic and speculative attitude to life, of the "sophistical pleasure of imagination", the "precious heart-stimulant of poetic illusion," "the snug delight of intellectual occupations". Since he was by nature both poet and philosopher, this was the mortification which the Christian law that "he that loseth his life shall save it" primarily implied for Kierkegaard.

By 'poetry' he seems to signify the romance of the youthful imagination and by 'speculation' the wisdom of this world. These are of time; real religion is of eternity: "poesy is youth, and worldly wisdom is the fruit of the years, and religiosity is the relation to the eternal" (U.P. p. 409). For him this was no mere pietistic gesture. Such a dying demanded the sacrifice of love; he paid the price. It meant the crucifixion of the erotic, aesthetic and philosophic desires of a profoundly passionate and gifted temperament and the abandonment of the role of 'genius' (which he knew himself by nature to be) for that of 'apostle'; from that mortification also he did not flinch.

It seems clear indeed that Kierkegaard really equates 'poesy' with romanticism; to 'poetize' is to romanticize. It is rather therefore romantic poetry and the romantic attitude to life and its substitution for religion by the Romantic movement, then so dominant and still so persistent, than poetry itself which he condemns. It is, for him, the lifeattitude of the 'first immediacy'. He seems to suggest, moreover, that not only he himself but European civilisation has come to the point when it must sacrifice such a romanticism or perish: "it seems", he wrote, "as though the age of poetry were past . . . That the age of poetry is past signifies that immediacy is no more" (St. pp. 74-5). He sensed, as so many have done since his day, the end of an age. But he was primarily concerned with the relation of such a 'poesy' to religion. "Poetry is idolatry refined", he declared. He believed that in the popular Christianity of his day, "Christ has been completely poetized." Therefore, for an existential Christianity, "a man must get out of the poetical and into the existential, the ethical." "Christianity is (thus) as good as done away with"; therefore, "a poet's heart must break." "Christianly conceived, every poet-existence is sin, the sin to poetize instead of to be."

Nevertheless, though Christianity thus implied for him the crucifixion of the poetry, philosophy and romance of the 'first immediacy', it also prefigured a poetry and romance of another order, 'not of this world.' In his discourses on the lilies and the birds published after his second conversion in 1848, he proclaimed his purpose "to make evident the conflict between poetry and Christianity." "In comparison with this [natural poetry]", he declared, Christianity "is prose." Yet, he adds, it is also "precisely the poetry of eternity" (L2. p. 211). He foresaw, though he himself hardly attained, a singing of the spirit-self, the "new song" of the "new man", of the "second immediacy." Moreover, from the pyre of unregenerate romance, the romance of the life of spirit soared like the phoenix. In a paper written in 1853 he writes lyrically of this new romance which dawns for him beyond the death of the old. Its refrain is "endlessly thou art loved."

Such was his self-criticism and self-mortification, his condemnation of himself and his world. But his drastic denials of the religion and culture of his world were no arm-chair onslaughts. His world-criticism is also self-criticism; "when I want to spit", he writes, "I spit in my own face." No student of his life can deny the truth of that statement. It was a severity to which the Erinyes, the furies of his fate, implacably compelled him. Only by the severest of judgements could he save his soul in its existential extremity. "To put an end to coquetry I had to introduce severity." And the severity which he had "proved on his pulses" to be the only cautery which could cure his own inner conflict, he believed to be that by which the Christianity of his day could also alone be cured. For, in his own soul, he beheld the microcosm and mirror of his world. "For Christianity there is only one solution – severity" he concluded. For himself and for his world he must find "religiousness absolute, of a different sort from that of the parsons." His mission to men was thus formed in the matrix of his own need and suffering. He believed that his was the task of "introducing the unconditional . . . to utter the cry of alarm". It was a cry which was first sounded in and to his own soul.

The anatomy of the life of spirit thus founded upon despair and death is stated most forcibly in his *Sickness unto Death*. The book dates from the year 1848, when at last he felt justified in speaking in his own name and abandoned the veil of anonymity which, for ten years after his conversion he had felt constrained to adopt. He is now no longer exploring or discussing; he utters forthright and freely his insight into the nature of dread and despair, of the life of spirit and faith, and the dialectic of the Christian tension.

The life of spirit which he expounds proceeds from an agony of consciousness which is itself a dying, to despair, from despair to that state of tension whence the flame of spirit (which is eternal life) is struck, and from that tension to the life of the lovers of God and so to the fruits of the Spirit, "love, joy, peace". "A believer", he declares, "is surely a lover, yea, of all lovers the most in love." It is upon that final and triumphant note and not, as is so often misconceived, in the long counterpoint of conflict and paradox, that Kierkegaard's real gospel comes to rest and his ultimate word is to be found.

But it is from an agony of awareness that this procession of spirit derives: "the more consciousness, the more intense the despair." From such a consciousness self and the will to choice proceed. "The more consciousness, the more will." The individual, the self, emerges in the 'instant' of choice from that chaos of consciousness upon which spirit broods.

This law of integration in the life of spirit is integral to Kierkegaard's thought. "The Christian heroism is to venture wholly to be oneself as an individual man, this definite individual man, alone before the face of God." It is a courage which demands not only decision, but also grace, the grace which "compels him to be the self he does not will to be."

But Kierkegaard is preaching much more than mere individualism. To become individual, a self, is to become 'concrete' and "to become concrete is a synthesis". The conscious man is a "synthesis of the infinite and the finite, of the temporal and the eternal, of freedom and necessity." That synthesis is the fusion of the tension and dialectic of sin and faith, despair and hope. It is a state to which few attain or, having attained, dare to endure: "many are called but few are chosen." It is, moreover, a state which an individualistic society consistently condemns: "in our age it is a crime to have spirit." Nevertheless true selfhood and spirit are indissoluble: "spirit is the self." And it is the state of true freedom: "the self is freedom." It is the only real freedom, but it is a freedom which a man buys with all that he has and is; few desire or find it. For as Nicholas Berdyaev has written, "man is a slave because freedom is difficult, whereas slavery is easy."

Yet this individual self "gained by the infinite abstraction from everything outward, this naked, abstract self", is not the final self; it is "the first form of the infinite self", embryo self and spirit, no more. And since it involves the deliberate choice of the tension of the life of faith, it is also the choice of a deeper despair than any to which the natural man is heir – a despair which "has something of the eternal in its dialectic." For it confronts the infinite and the eternal and partakes of that which it confronts.

Here is the "sickness unto death", an "agonizing contradiction . . . everlastingly to die, to die and yet not to die."

It is so because the self is, in its essence, potentially eternal. Thus "despair has entered into something which cannot burn". Here we stand upon sub-Christian ground. It is the faith of Plotinus, with his "nothing that has being is destroyed"; the faith of the Bhagavad-Gîta, "never the spirit was born; the spirit shall cease to be never." It is the point at which much modern theosophy comes to rest.

But for Kierkegaard, with his Christian pre-suppositions, such despair, being a phenomenon of spirit, merges into faith. It is, as he wrote elsewhere in his journals, "that dialectical hovering which, though in fear and trembling, never despairs." In that dialectic is the paradox upon which all his thought and faith are poised. Here is the real Christian tension, the frontier between despair and faith.

The faith which thus polarizes despair is itself eternal life. In the field of that faith we pass from sub-Christian lowlands to Christian summits. For the humanist *Cogito ergo sum*, "I think therefore I am", Kierkegaard substitutes the Christian counter-creed, "to believe is to be." Belief is being. The former lives the soul-life of natural consciousness and becoming, a life transient and perishable as the flowers of the field, the other the imperishable spirit-life of being.

None the less, for our frontier state of mortality it is a faith which remains subject to the dialectic, tension and paradox whence it derives. The Christian, so Kierkegaard conceives, swings ever between faith and unfaith; his faith too is a 'swinging wicket'.

"To reach truth one must pierce through every negativity." Faith and doubt are thus linked in this humanly indissoluble dialectic. For Kierkegaard as for Emerson, "a saint is a sceptic once in every twenty-four hours."

But beyond that "swinging-wicket" of despair and faith is that land of light where God's lovers live in an "immediacy", a new spontaneity of reborn spirit, of which the immediacy of sense is but the reflection in time. So we reach Kierkegaard's "fundamental formula" for the life of spirit: "by relating itself to its own self and by willing to be itself the self is grounded *transparently* in the Power which posited it." It is "grounded *transparently*"; Kierkegaard strains towards the dim concept of that life of the person-self or spirit, reborn from the death of the self of nature, crystal-clear, the mirror of Eternal Being, the state of saints, which is the lodestar of his "troubled truth."

Such are the dark foundations of the starry faith to which Kierkegaard's existential thinking impelled him – faith in a life of spirit (eternal life) rooted in the dialectic of despair and faith, despair which is itself sin and yet (*O felix culpa*, "O blissful guilt"!) the occasion of redemption, the sin which, so he declares in defiance of the humanists, "lies in the will, not in the intellect." For the Christian, he contends, it must be so, for the self born from despair is confronted with Christ, and since "a self is quantitatively what its measure is", therefore the law of spirit that "the more self the more intense the sin" comes into fatal force.

It is a despair-born faith with an obvious relevance for our own day of despair. Kierkegaard diagnoses the dialectic of such despair with an unequalled acumen. But he does more than diagnose; he points towards a Christianity of the spirit beyond a decomposing Christianity of the soul, an eternal life beyond the 'tragic climax' of the life of nature. "First death, then life"; his own laconic aphorism is the pith of his faith; he believed it to be the pith of the Gospel.

Progress, or regress, to real religion was thus for Kierkegaard a series of 'stages', 'spheres' or 'categories'. He has variously enumerated these. "There are three stages: an aesthetic, an ethical, and a religious" (U.P. p. 261). "The spheres are thus related: immediacy; finite common sense;

irony; ethics with irony as incognito; and then finally the Christian religiousness" (U.P. p. 473. note). These 'stages' or 'spheres' are milestones upon his existential progress from the life-attitude of the natural man, the poet or aesthete, to that of the man of God as he observed them in his own case. His 'categories' – the individual, dread, guilt, repetition, the "instant" – are a specifically inward and religious differentiation. The first three lead him to the threshold of real religion. Recognition of individual selfhood leads to dread and despair, dread to the sense of guilt before God, guilt to a dying to the natural self and to the repetition of that self in the spirit-self re-born in the 'instant' which is eternal life.

It was at this stage of the consciousness of guilt – the period of his father's confession and death, his breach with Regina and the "great earthquake" of his first conversion – that he grasped the category of what he called 'repetition'. Although conditioned by his own emotional catastrophe, it was in the first place as an intellectual concept that it came to him. For one who lived so much in the mind it was perhaps inevitable that a mental should precede a moral reversal. Repetition was thus for mind what conversion and regeneration are for soul. Kierkegaard was to carry that transformation from the life of mind to that of spirit, but it was in terms of thought that it must first be seized. For the 'intellectual', which he then predominantly was, the temptation to arrest that conversion within a mind insulated from life must have been immense; it is the mark of his calibre that he could not be content till he had lived what he had thought.

It is in this concept of repetition that the clue to Kierkegaard's reconception of Christianity is to be found. It is also here that his message comes with a special relevance to that class of 'intellectuals' who are so numerous in latter-day European culture. For such citizens of the 'kingdom of the mind' a Christianity couched in terms of emotion or morality makes no immediate appeal. They too must first be converted in mind if Christianity is to have meaning for them. The concept of repetition implies such a conversion of mind – a reversed life-view. In his book *Repetition* Kierkegaard gave to the world an intellectual's 'pilgrim's progress' or regress.

But though it leads to a primarily intellectual *volte face*, the book was forged in his personal emotional agony. He had realized, as he wrote in his journal, that he was "an eternity too old for" Regina. None the less the poet and romantic in him mourned for her loss and, recollecting his "first, fine, careless rapture" of love, longed for its repetition. In that very recollection he finds only the "rank weed of memory" which "strangled every thought at birth". It is notable that it is *thought* rather than feeling which is strangled. It was thus in his thinking that he is first driven to seek deliverance. For if he could no longer think he could no longer live. By nature and nurture he was a disciple of Descartes. So fate forced melancholy to despair. While he waits and hopes, Regina marries; and, with a devastating disillusionment, he finds that "all his sentiments were bosh", and in that despair finds the type of all human despair. The "melancholy of repetition" is a mirage; repetition seems no more than myth.

The Regina episode precipitated a conflict which had long been latent; it was primarily a conflict of attitudes. "His nature", he writes, "had become split." He is two beings, the 'observer', whom he names 'Constantine Constantius', who tells the tale and the young man in love of whom the tale is told. These two selves contend within him and typify his own conflicting life-attitudes. The 'observer' is the "cold disciple of reflection", a stoic armed against immediate contact with life with the "elasticity of irony", who can stand aside from life and view it dispassionately. It was a pose natural and congenial to the young poet and philosopher, and one which, in his reprobate phase, he had deliberately cultivated. But the 'observer' avoids existential experience of life, therefore he cannot comprehend a religion relevant for reality. For Kierkegaard now perceives that it is only when "Stoicism has stepped aside" that a man is confronted with religious decision. And now, for him, nothing short of real religion can suffice his need.

In the 'observer' Kierkegaard is thus embodying the detached, speculative thought, culture and religiosity which he was so fiercely to assail in the professors, dons and parsons whom he denounced. The ferocity of the attack is the measure of his realization of his own participation in the guilt which he condemned. He was castigating the speculative philosopher, the romantic poet, the ineffectual don, the unrealist parson in himself. He was, in fact, denouncing the *trahison des clercs*, the betrayal of life and the unlettered by the intellectuals which Julian Benda condemned in our own day. For Kierkegaard that betrayal lay precisely in this aesthetic, philosophic, religious detachment from real life to which he himself was peculiarly prone. It is again a diagnosis of intellectualism which anticipated the modern repudiation of the 'highbrow'. But where most modern criticism of that disease of spirit can only condemn, Kierkegaard probes to its roots in himself and, from his own agony of self-awareness, wrests what he conceives to be the remedy.

His passion was too poignant, his despair too deep, his integrity too steely to permit him to take any final refuge in the adoption of such an 'observer' role towards life and love. The lover in him could not thus be repressed. In this intense inner drama the simple humanity of the "young man in love" is thrown into sharp contrast to the 'observer'.

His 'immediacy' cannot be quelled with Stoicism; he must live, not look on at life. He retains, against all that "pure reason" may contend, his original 'immediacy', his direct contact with life, as, within Kierkegaard's own intellectual detachment, passion burned on. Like Job, the lover will not renounce his 'integrity' or decline the conflict of life and love. He continues to yearn for the repetition of first love and to bear the brunt of recollection's melancholy and despair. Like Job, he endures to the end of his agony and bewilderment and accepts a probation which he cannot comprehend. Like Job, he receives his answer. It is, as for Job, the answer of neither logic nor morality; it is the reality of repetition.

This conflict of consciousness, so modern in grain, is so poignantly conveyed as, for the reader aware of what is involved, to be almost intolerable. The failure of love takes the dimensions of failure in life. When raised, as Kierkegaard must raise it, to the level of metaphysics and religion, the melancholy of recollection becomes such a despair and life-loathing as that which darkens the tragic period of Shakespeare. Mere recollection becomes a nightmare; the 'repetition' dimly surmised is beyond his reach. The tension can only be relieved by a 'thunderstorm' – an act of God – for he knows himself to be at the end of his powers. The storm breaks; he learns that Regina is married; "it came as a thunderstorm after all."

The 'thunderstorm' spells for Kierkegaard transcendence and miracle. It is that which cleaves the skies of his consciousness from beyond his ken or his expectation. The stroke which, through no volition of his own, destroys his 'first immediacy' and annihilates his dreams of repetition of love, also reveals to him the nature of the 'second immediacy', the spontaneity of the 'new man' and the nature of a real repetition. His cleft consciousness is suddenly made whole. "I am again myself", he writes, "here I have the repetition, I understand everything, and existence seems more beautiful than ever." "The discord in my nature is resolved, I am again unified."

In this experience of repetition he knows the double benediction of Job; all that he had counted lost he finds again. He has regained his very self, his very life, out of despair and death. It is indeed a double boon, for not only has he found the 'new man', but he has regained the 'old man' reborn; he knows both 'immediacies', that of innocence and that of experience, in memory and in faith, in recollection and in repetition. But it is repetition in the sphere of spirit, not of flesh; "only spiritual repetition is possible." It is of eternity, not of time; "eternity . . . is the true repetition." So he can go forward, in "fear and trembling", yet "rejoicing in repetition".

Such an acutely personal experience must remain, in the main, incommunicable. Its reality can only be gauged by its results. Although emotional in origin, it was, as has been noted, at this stage chiefly as an intellectual illumination that the concept of repetition burst upon Kierkegaard's brain. Had it remained so it might well be dismissed as self-dramatization. But it did not; what he saw in mind, he lived out in person. And here is the soil from which his faith flowers. It is from this experience that his conviction of the transcendence of God seems to be derived. For he is utterly sure that the revelation which has come upon him is unconditioned and uncaused by any human causation. Like Cortez on Darien he gazes upon a new world. It is a new world of the spirit and eternity which he hails with an amazed exultation eloquent of profound conviction.

It is thus as a new vision of the meaning of life in the mind that, at first and in this book, he experiences this *volte face*, this reversal of attitude. "Repetition is a new category", he declares, a new world-view. The full significance of the Christian world-view has suddenly dawned upon his mind and he realizes the complete reversal of conception and attitude which it implies. "Recollection is the pagan life-view; repetition is the modern life view", he writes. By 'modern' he evidently means 'Christian'. "Recollection" affirms that "all that is has been"; it can therefore never be repeated; "the things which I have seen I now can see no more" (Wordsworth). "Repetition", on the other hand, "affirms that existence which has been now becomes." Essence and existence, being and becoming, are made one in Christ. For Being, the Alpha and the Omega, the eternal Christ, becomes in time and flesh. Thus, in the category of repetition, "we look before and after and pine", not for "what is not" (as for Shelley and in pagan recollection), but for what "was, is and evermore shall be", by virtue of the Incarnation. The category of repetition is thus the category of the incarnate Christ.

Here is the Christian paradox which is the 'absurd' of faith, but it is a paradoxical faith which illuminates life, out of despair begets conviction and from futility meaning. He labours almost breathlessly to enumerate the attributes and implications of this Christian repetition. "It signifies freedom"; "it is consciousness raised to the second power"; it is "a *sine-qua-non* of every dogmatic problem"; it is "always a transcendence." "True repetition is eternity"; it is "to receive oneself again"; it is "the life of spirit" in which "the germinal sprout comes last" (thus reversing the order of natural life); it is peace, for the "religious individual" which repetition creates "reposes in himself." In fact for Kierkegaard the category of repetition implies the second Eden, the "immediacy of the new man."

Here then is the crux of his existential Christianity, the watershed which divides the pagan from the Christian life-view. For in such Christian repetition the *Ave atque Vale*, "hail and farewell", to life characteristic of the pagan (and pseudo-Christian) attitude to life is reversed to a Christian

Vale atque Ave, "farewell and hail". In the recollection of the former attitude man can only look back with an infinite regret to the first Eden of his unfallen state, of his innocency. But the Christian who knows repetition looks both back and forward. Recollection is thus the mode of immanence, repetition that of transcendence.

Thus out of the affirmation of the individual self which, when confronted with reality, begets dread and, when confronted with Christ, guilt, dawns the third category of repetition, and in that transition the foundations of Kierkegaard's faith are laid. It is as yet a faith of concept rather than conduct, and one of which the implications have yet to be lived out. But, having attained to this category of repetition, Kierkegaard knows his direction. He has heard his "word"; in the doing of that "word" he learns the doctrine of that Christianity of the spirit which remains to be explored.

4

Inwardness and the Instant

KIERKEGAARD'S existential rediscovery of Christianity led him to a religion of 'inwardness' and the spirit, to, in the terms of St. Paul's antinomy, a rejection of a Christianity 'after the flesh' – a Christianity come to terms with the life of this world – and the search for a Christianity 'after the spirit'. A religious realism which began with a realistic acceptance of human conditions of time and 'the flesh' led, by its own inexorable logic, to an absolute necessity for their fulfilment, transcension and transformation in the life of spirit. For a candid confrontation of those conditions and of the 'inwardness' of the human heart reveal a profound conflict and contradiction within them, a 'law of Abraxas',[1] a "grain of evil seed sown in the heart of Adam from the beginning", a "leaven of unrighteousness" by reason of which, in their own unredeemed cycle of causality, they come, in the end, to an inevitable corruption. 'Flesh', save for 'spirit', is doomed. But the reality of spirit is reached, not in spite of, but through and beyond the reality of 'the flesh'. There is the core of Kierkegaard's reconception of Christianity. It was not a new but an old treasure of Christian truth newly interpreted.

Only a conception of spirit at least as concrete and realistic as the conditions and sin which it transcends and saves could suffice for such a salvation. Kierkegaard's Christianity is thus rooted in a profound realism. For him such a realism implied an inwardness growing continually more searching and intense. For he could not forget that "the kingdom of

[1] "The law of contradiction in all man's sublunary aims" (*Secular Despair and Christian Faith*; by Alec Vidler. p. 18).

Heaven is *within*." It is a realism so distasteful to man, for
whom the outward life is familiar and secure but the inward
obscure and haunted, that only a catastrophe threatening his
very existence can compel the soul to confront it. Such a
catastrophe cleft Kierkegaard's own 'inwardness'; to-day it
assails our world both without and within. In the space of a
century the conflict and calamity which he divined within
the soul of Western man have become externalized in a
chaos of world-conditions. That is his real significance for
our time. It is when we read his inward agony with refer-
ence to the radical revolution in which we live that the
study of the man kindles into a biting pertinence for the
problems which beset us.

His main and constant 'cry of alarm' is 'look within'.
But his conception of 'inwardness' is far removed from
quietism or a pietistic spirituality; it is a passionately concerned intensity which is the seed-plot of spirit. "Christianity is spirit, spirit is inwardness, inwardness is subjectivity,
subjectivity is essentially passion and in its maximum an
infinite, personal, passionate interest in one's eternal happiness" (U.P. p. 33). The statement is one which calls for
comment from the context of his other utterances. For
Kierkegaard is constantly conscious that his experience is
microcosmic, that his private happiness or suffering are also,
in some sense, those of mankind; his preoccupation with his
own inner drama has always this universal connotation.
His real concern is always rather with man than self, but his
existentialism implied that it was in the study of himself
that he could best know mankind. Moreover it is no un-
sanctified but a holy and disciplined passion which he com-
mends – a passion for the truth, for Christ, God only and
eternal life. For what he termed 'unshaven passion' – the
passion of the unbridled senses – he held no brief.

Thus the essential impulse of real religion is for him a
passionate and personal concern. And passion is suffering.

"Passion implies pathos, an infinite susceptibility to suffer-ing . . . action in inwardness is suffering . . . it is for this reason that suffering is the highest form of inwardness" (U.P. p. 388). Thus inwardness spells a suffering growing ever more intense as inwardness drives more deep. It is no interior life guarded and secluded from life's storms and actuality, but a deepening, through an existential experi-ence neither denied nor despised but embraced to the uttermost, to the essence of existence, to the quick of consciousness.

Inwardness therefore involves risk. "Without risk there is no faith, the greater the risk the greater the faith; the more objective security the less inwardness" (U.P. p. 188). "Faith is precisely the contradiction between the infinite passion of the individual's inwardness and the objective un-certainty. If I am capable of grasping God objectively, I do not believe, but precisely because I cannot do this I must believe" (U.P. 182). Inwardness demands daring: "to dare . . . is Christianity." His characteristic simile for this venture of inwardness and faith is that of the deep sea. To be "in danger, above seventy fathoms of water, many miles from all help, there to be joyful – that is great" (S.E. p. 425). For him, a real Christianity involves embarking upon an ocean of intellectual and spiritual uncertainty and abandon-ment of the safe ports of probability. "All religious (not to say Christian) adventure is on the further side of probability, is by letting go of probability" (S.E. p. 116).

It is significant that Kierkegaard's instinct should have chosen the simile of the sea; for modern psychology, then in its infancy, like primordial mythology, finds in the sea the universal archetype for the unconscious; it was from the 'great waters' of the underworld that Babylonian mythology derived life and wisdom. For that which Kier-kegaard styles 'inwardness' evidently in part corresponds to that which modern psychology calls the unconscious or the subconscious. He plumbed indeed to depths of spirit far below the levels of the psyche to which psychology as such can do no more than point, but that inward Odyssey, being existential, traversed regions of the subconscious to which then there was no map.

In his own existential experience he had known to his cost the perilous nature of that quest – the demonic forces of the unconscious released in such an inwardness which psychology has since more fully revealed. "What the inner voice brings close to us", Professor C. G. Jung has lately written, "is generally something that is not good, but evil ... In a most unaccountable way the lowest and the highest, the best and the most atrocious, the truest and the falsest are mingled together in the inner voice, which opens up to us an abyss of confusion, deception and despair" (*The Integration of Personality*, passim). Such are the perils of inwardness; Kierkegaard knew them well. It is for fear of them he held, that men take shelter in the security of convention, objectivity and abstract dogma which, to quote Professor Jung again, "advises us not to have an unconscious." But Kierkegaard, believing with Lascelles Abercrombie that in the religious life, "prudence is the deadly sin", scorned such securities of soul.

These were perils, now in some degree known and charted, which Kierkegaard braved a century ago. He did not escape unscathed. "I only have", he writes in his journal, "pale, bloodless, hard-lived midnight shapes to fight against to which I myself give life and existence." He is pursued by dread and lives his inner life in a constant 'fear and trembling.' "It [dread] grips me with its terror," he confesses, "I cannot and must not flee from it, I must endure the thought; then I find a religious composure and then I am as free and happy as spirit" (St. p. 340). "The whole content of my being shrieks in contradiction against itself" (R. p. 114-5). These are symptoms to which modern psychiatry is accustomed. Kierkegaard confronted them without the aids of psychiatry and found his cure in 'God only'.

In the light of modern psychological research Kierkegaard's doctrine and practice of inwardness thus assume in some degree the character of an extension of the Christian consciousness into the regions of the subconscious. With a remarkable pre-view of our own new awareness of those 'great waters' below the surface of our conscious life, it is as though he both sought and carried the Cross into that underworld and, in daring that perilous descent into his own inwardness, followed his Lord into a 'nether world', a *She'ôl* of the soul to which then there was no Christian chart. He thus obeyed the injunction of another master of instinctive Christian psychology, St. Augustine – *descendite ut ascendatis*, "descend that you may ascend".

His intuition of the need for such an inwardness was in itself prophetic. He seems to have been aware of an impending crisis in the history of the human consciousness, that Western civilization was nearing (it is now a commonplace) the 'end of an age' and doomed either to a new mutation or to destruction. He saw that the crust of our culture, morality and religion, had become too brittle to contain the mounting inner fires; he proclaimed the 'bankruptcy of Europe' and the danger of a demonic possession which has now passed into history. He was convinced that Christianity alone could control that chaos, but only a Christianity with the courage to descend and confront it in the inward world, and that the established religion of his day was selling the passes of Christendom for the sake of comfort and security. It is a diagnosis which many have made to-day. "Everywhere else", as Peter Drucker wrote in *The End of Economic Man* in 1940, "demonic forces roam outside the natural order."

Such a psychological view of Kierkegaard's word and

work explains much that otherwise seems obscure – the in-comprehension and hostility of a church which either would not or could not face the uncomfortable vistas to which he pointed, the mounting violence of his denuncia-tion of an unrealism which, to his insight, was dastardly and incomprehensible, the stubborn attempt of vested interests in church and state to discount the dangerous discredit to their status which his prophecy implied and to muffle his cry of alarm. For man fears nothing so much as the unknown, and they who live, both eco-nomically and spiritually, by the church are very loth to admit that its fabric is rotten. It is more comfortable to dwell in the past than to face a menacing future, and to cultivate the sown lands of the conscious than to explore the wilds of the subconscious. Churchmen can be as tena-cious of spiritual as laymen of economic security. Kierke-gaard had looked into deeps of the soul of which his con-temporaries were either unaware or afraid; he could not go back, and they dared not go forward.

A century later the inwardness of which he was then a solitary pathfinder and herald has become an acknowledged and, to some extent, an explored area of the human psyche. But it has not yet been christianized, and it seems as true to-day as when Kierkegaard wrote that a Christianity which fails in that mission will have only a failing message for a world now forced into awareness of the facts which he foretold. Can Christianity overcome that inward world also? Such seems to be the essential challenge of Kierke-gaard's doctrine of inwardness to the Christianity of our own as of his day. He proclaimed triumphantly that it could, but only at the price of a new and costly awareness, inwardness and religious realism.

From such an angle many of what might otherwise seem unjustifiable over-emphases in his writings become under-standable. He saw that venture of inwardness as a quite blind 'leap in the dark'; for him it was so. And he believed that only a rare knightly heroism of spirit could undertake it; for such a pioneer venture into an unknown dimension it was and always is so. Such forerunners are ever "knights of infinity", Don Quixotes of the spirit, knights "of reflection . . . of the sorrowful countenance". It was indeed only such a reckless and knightly courage which could then dare such a 'leap' from the security of the conscious to the unknown deeps of the subconscious, from the dimension of soul to that of spirit, from rational and dogmatic proofs and probabilities to the 'absurd' and the 'offence' of faith-knowledge.

He is very insistent upon the "yawning abyss" between these opposites. "There is no direct transition (by logical proof)", he writes, "to the thing of becoming a Christian." "Faith is against understanding, faith is on the other side of death." And becoming Christian and faith were, for Kierkegaard, coterminous with inwardness. For him the only *vraie vérité*, the ultimate Truth, was inward. Therefore a Christianity confined to the extroverted life, the beaten tracks of consciousness and tradition and the security of convention, were for him utterly unreal. Therefore for him "Christianity doesn't exist" (S.E. p. 155).

Such intransigent declarations are characteristic of Kierkegaard's prophecy. They are doubtless in part to be attributed to his sense of urgency and the need for stabbing the Christianity of his time 'broad awake'. Prophecy and prudence rarely march together. But from the angle of the psychological *éclaircissement* since his day which has been considered, it seems possible for a balanced modern criticism to mitigate his condemnation of 'once-born', conventional and conservative Christianity, his emphasis upon the almost impossible heroism required for the venture of faith, and the gulf between rational and faith knowledge. In a fully catholic Christianity there is room for both the once- and the twice-born types of piety, for extroverted and conservative and for an introverted and creative Christianity; it is a wisdom which is "justified of all her children." The conquest of the subconscious is no longer altogether the 'forlorn hope' which it was for Kierkegaard, and the gulf between rational and faith-knowledge perhaps less unbridgeable than he assumed.

Such considerations, though they may discount some over-emphasis, do not minimize the fortitude of spirit which such a venture of faith and inwardness implied for Kierkegaard in his "pre-psychological" age, or the significance and relevance of his conception of a Christianity of inwardness for an age committed either to a conquest of its own subconscious forces or to conquest by them. And while psychology wrestles with this crucial problem of the underworld of the soul of man, established Christianity to-day seems as prone to evade the issue as in his day in Denmark.

But his conception of inwardness has far more than a merely psychological content; it plumbs to deeper levels than those of the soul of man. His real and ultimate wrestling was upon the plane of spirit. He affirmed that "the movement of the spirit was inward," that "Christianity is precisely an affair of spirit, and so of subjectivity, and so of inwardness", and that "to be spirit – this is man's invisible glory." Psychology can only analyse and diagnose the diseases of the soul; the synthesis, the making whole, healthy, holy of the soul is in the power of spirit alone. "Into this night of hopelessness", he wrote in 1851 when he had "ventured far out" in the life of spirit, "comes then the life-giving Spirit and brings hope, for according to that merely natural hope there was no hope left, and so this is hope against hope" (S.E. p. 101). It is at this point, therefore, that he has a word still more relevant for our condition for which even the 'new psychology' can offer no cure. Kierkegaard pointed to an inwardness more profound than that of psychology and proclaimed (what Christianity has always professed) that the only salvation for soul is spirit.

In this deep spiritual inwardness it would seem that Kierkegaard is of the company of the great Christian mystics. Yet the name of mystic was one which he hotly repudiated. For mysticism, as he conceived it, was a short-cut to salvation for which a real Christianity gave no warrant. He rejects with an equal ardour all claim to a mystical revelation on his own part. "I beg the reader", he writes in his autobiographical sketch *The Point of View*, "not to think of revelations or anything of the sort, for with me everything is dialectical." He will not admit to any moment of mystical unity or ecstasy; for him all spiritual experience is strictly conditioned and subject to the tensions, dialectic and paradox of mortal life. The 'unitive state' which some forms of mysticism claim in the flesh is for him an arrogant defiance of the dualism which constituted man's divinely appointed probation in time.

Yet the journal entries which describe his moments of conversion suggest experiences as mystical as those recounted in similar terms by St. Paul or Pascal. In 1838 he writes, "There is an indescribable joy which kindles us as inexplicably as the apostle's outburst", and in 1848, "My whole nature is changed . . . I must speak" (J. 207 & 747). These are utterances with the authentic mystical ring. What Rudolf Otto has called "first-type mysticism . . . withdrawal from all outward things, retreat into the ground of one's own soul, knowledge of the secret depth and the possibility of turning in upon one's self" seems altogether consonant with Kierkegaard's experience and doctrine of inwardness.

A few of the characteristic sayings of the great mystics, moreover, suffice to demonstrate the affinity between Kierkegaard's inwardness and such mysticism. "The secret way lies inward . . . the swiftest steed to bear you to your goal is suffering; none shall ever taste eternal bliss but those who stand with Christ in depths of bitterness "(Eckhart). "By love may he be gotten and holden but by thought never" (*The Cloud of Unknowing*). "God works in us from within outwards . . . we must all found our lives upon a fathomless abyss" (Ruysbroek). "He made his understanding blind, not venturing to apply an instrument so vile to a matter so high"; "I die because I do not die" (St. John-of-the-Cross). Such sayings evidently speak the very language of Kierkegaard and echo his thought.

If the mystic, as the derivation of the word denotes, is one who closes lips, eyes and ears to outward things that he may look and hear within, then Kierkegaard's Christianity of inwardness must be classed as of the true mystical tradition. But with a more vaunting and specious form of mysticism which denies the reality of the ostensible world and the self, and claims immediate union with Deity, Kierkegaard has nothing in common. His repudiation of mysticism seems, indeed, like many more of his more trenchant utterances, to be rather a corrective of a false than denial of a true theology. In the proper, though not in the Christianly improper sense of the term, he was a mystic. He seeks and finds reality within, and Schweitzer's conclusion that "all logical thinking ends in mysticism" seems accurately to describe his own attitude towards all speculative philosophy and dogmatic theology.

The inwardness which Kierkegaard sought was thus no fantasy-world escaping from the conditions of human existence but that of a reality more real and profound than the established Christianity of his day could comprehend. Of an escapist inwardness he writes with the full edge of his irony, of pseudo-Christians "christianly keeping their Christianity in hidden inwardness and employing their natural gifts and talents to succeed in the world" (T.C. p. 219). And again, "One should deny oneself in hidden inwardness, in hidden inwardness renounce the world and all that is of the world, but (for God's sake! shall I say?) one must not let it be observed. In this way established Christianity becomes a collection of what one might call honorary Christians" (T.C. p. 246).

Kierkegaard's doctrine of inwardness is thus, in Professor W. E. Hocking's phrase, that of a "deepening to the essence" of Christianity, below soul to spirit, below becoming to being. It was a religion of the essence, the inward being, of life that he conceived Christianity to be. It was thus not only the unconditional which he sought through and beyond conditioned existence but also, through time, the eternal. For him inwardness and the "instant" were of the same eternal order. But, so he tirelessly reiterates, there are for man no short cuts to that state of essence, being, spirit, eternal life. To reach the unconditioned one must, in Charles Lamb's wise words, "accept one's conditions"; to attain to eternal life one must accept the limitations of time. An inwardness which pretended to despise the conditions of mortal life, a mysticism which claimed eternal life within our mortal time, were equally anathema to his conception of Christianity. It is, again, in that existential realism that he speaks the idiom of our own age and with that conception of a Christianity of the spirit seen only, in St. Augustine's phrase, "through the lattice of our flesh" that he offers the cure for its disease.

At root the two conceptions meet. For Kierkegaard the 'instant' was "not an atom of time but of eternity." But it flowers in the womb of time. "It is short, indeed, and temporal, as every instant is, gone like all instants, the following instant, and yet it is decisive, and yet it is full of eternity. Such an instant must have a special name, let us call it *the fullness of time*" (L. pp. 121 & 312). It is a conception which anticipates much modern speculation upon the relation of time and eternity. In his Bampton lectures on Time and Eternity in Christian Thought, Dr. F. H. Brabant conceived of eternity in the same sense: "In the deepest and truest sense of the word 'Eternity', we find that the emphasis is much less upon lastingness or duration than upon completeness or perfection."

Moreover, for Kierkegaard, the 'instant', like inwardness, also implies the 'leap' of faith. "The instant does not need to be long, for it is a leap", he writes. And, like inwardness, it also implies paradox. "If only the Instant is posited, the Paradox is granted." "An instant", comments Dr. Lowrie, "if it is only an instant in time, is 'filled with emptiness'. What fills it with eternity is the apprehension of the paradox that God became man. It is then the decisive Instant of faith." And that instant is eternity; it is the instant of 're-petition' in which past, present and future are fused in an 'immortal moment'.

It is a conception which, like that of inwardness, is constant and crucial for Kierkegaard. It was by this name that he called the series of pamphlets with which in 1855, the year of his death, he launched his attack upon the established church. This for him was what "to work in the instant" had come to mean; it is characteristic of the man and his thought that he should have envisaged his own ultimate 'instant' in the terms of a strictly conditioned task – that of disabusing his generation of "the illusion of being Christians and the belief that the parson's game of Christianity is Christianity" (L. p. 577). There, at last, lay his own "leap in the dark", his decisive, existential 'instant'. It synchronized with his leap into the darkness of death.

For Kierkegaard the 'instant' thus implied, as the derivation of the word infers, a standing within. It is the opposite of 'ecstasy', a standing outside of existence. Kierkegaard's Christianity was one of instancy, not ecstasy. In the instant a man, standing within his time and existence, takes his stand in the immutable and eternal essence or being which underlie them. Existence is a standing out or forth from that pure being; the instant is a return to it, a standing within it. Thus the existential movement, according to Kierkegaard, is from and through existence to the "instant", and that movement is one of inwardness. Both conceptions turn, like the compass-needle to the north, to the 'still Centre' of our time and existence.

For him that conversion or turning again to the soul's true north is essentially what he called "the thing of becoming a Christian"; for Christianity and for him, that true north, that 'still Centre' of the instant was, as for St. Paul, *in* Christ. But since our life here is a life of becoming, he dare not affirm that he is, only that he seeks and hopes to become a Christian. The instant is thus a fundamental Christian category. Paul Claudel wrote that "Eternity and Resurrection are ceaselessly renewed in the Instant" (*Le Père Humilié*), and in that saying epitomized what seems to have been the significance of this conception of the "instant" for Kierkegaard. In that instant the inward and the eternal meet in a timeless here-and-now reached through and within, yet ever beyond, our space-time continuum. There is the point of intersection where the longtitudinal line of human life, love (*eros*), thought and time meet the vertical line of eternity and the downpouring love (*agape*) of God. For the Christian, for Kierkegaard, that instant of intersection, is the cross of the incarnate Christ. There is the paradox of faith.

His conception of this inward meeting of time and eternity in an Instant filled with eternity, the fulfilment and perfection of time and existence, is one which grows increasingly salient in modern thought and feeling. It has been echoed and expressed in lapidary language by T. S. Eliot in his group of war-born poems, *Four Quartets*. For Eliot as for Kierkegaard, reality and eternity meet within at "the still point of the turning world" and –

F

> "The point of intersection of the timeless
>   With time . . ."

For each the way to that instant lies inward:

> "into another intensity
>   For a further union, a deeper communion".

And for each that way lies —

> "Through the dark cold and the empty desolation . . ."

And for each the apprehension (or in Kierkegaard's language, the 'appropriation') of that "timeless moment" "is the occupation for a saint". The categories of inwardness, repetition and the instant alike, for Kierkegaard, point to the necessity for sanctity and the life of spirit in existence. That is the only way to eternal life; it is the way of inwardness. It was a way which he strove to follow "not only in lip but in life". In the doing he learned his doctrine of the life of spirit.

5

The Way and the Life

KIERKEGAARD'S reconception of Christianity led him from, in his own terms, 'reflection' to the 'new immediacy', from the region of abstract speculation to that of a dynamic and concrete faith, and from faith to following, to a way and a life. That process from thought to deed and faith to following is implicit in his existentialism, and it is in obedience to its intrinsic logic that, as he matures, his writings become increasingly concerned with, not the theory, but the practice of the presence of God.

For his chief 'corrective' to a Christianity for which 'pure faith' (like 'pure reason') had become increasingly escapist and unreal was his passionate affirmation that "belief is being." With that truth he sought to salve the fatal spirit-matter, faith-works, contemplation-action, religious-secular dualism which, so he conceived, divided and paralysed Christendom at its source. He was not content to diagnose that disease and propound its Christian cure; he applied his 'corrective' to his own Christian living. From the date of his second conversion in 1848 till his death seven years later his prime concern is with the Christian life, the personal 'appropriation' of Christian truth and the application of his faith to his own conditions.

That faith had, indeed, originated in 'reflection' as an intellectual revelation, a world-view. But it had been forged in passion, not only of thought but also of feeling; the tempered blade was not merely a formula for mind but a living force for life. Since for him faith thus implied living and believing being, faith was also for him a thing never finished but always, like life itself, in process of becoming. Therefore he disclaimed the possession of faith just as he disclaimed the name of Christian. "I have constantly said",

he wrote, " 'I have not faith' – like a bird's anxious flight
before the approaching tempest, so I have expressed the
presentiment of stormy confusion; I have not faith . . .
there sits in a cloister cell like Luther, or in a remote cham-
ber, a solitary man in fear and trembling. There indeed lies
the truth" (S.E. p. 44).

Thus for Kierkegaard faith itself is existential – neither
intellectual assent nor dogmatic acquiescence, but a life:
"faith is a new life" (T.C. p. 121). It is "immediacy after
reflection", the "second immediacy" of the "new man."
Being a mode of life and not merely of thought, it is rooted
in existential passion. "Faith is a passion", he declared, "the
highest passion in the sphere of human subjectivity"
(U.P. p. 118). It is a passion, not prudence, and therefore,
like all passion, ready for risk; he speaks of the "foolhardi-
ness of faith." "Without risk there is no faith, and the greater
the risk the greater the faith" (U.P. 118).

He thus shares with Pascal the conception of faith as a
wager. The object of that wager of faith is "the absurd" –
the fact that "the eternal truth has come into being in time,
that God has come into being." For Kierkegaard it is precisely this 'leap' beyond reason, this wager upon 'the
absurd', which constitutes Christian faith. More, it is the
task of faith to seek 'the absurd.' "Faith has two tasks: to take
care in every moment to discover the improbable, the paradox; and then to hold it fast with the passion of inwardness"
(U.P. p. 209). Just as true Christianity requires a reversal,
conversion, *volte face* in life, so in mind; as the 'new life' is
contrary to the old life of flesh, so those who are "renewed
in the spirit of [their] minds" base their thinking upon pro-
positions which are paradoxical and absurd to unregenerate
reason. They must not only accept, they must seek for a
truth which offends the natural mind and the 'laws of
thought.' For "reason cannot grasp what faith believes"
(J. 1033).

This emphasis upon the paradoxical and the absurd must, for a catholic criticism, be gauged in consideration of Kierkegaard's reaction from the prevalent rationalism of his day and his urgent sense of the need for a 'corrective' which, if it were to disturb complacency, could not be couched in moderate terms. It was not his task, as he conceived it, to seek for a synthesis or *summa* of rational and faith knowledge, but to declare that which the thought and theology of his day tended to deny, that between human reason and divine truth a great gulf is fixed, that it is not by "taking thought" that man finds God, that faith is infinitely removed from mere intellectual assent or doctrine. "The object of faith is not a doctrine," he declares, "but God's reality in existence as a particular individual" (U.P. p. 290).

Since the object of faith is itself a "living God", the faith which meets such a God must also itself be a vital process, dynamic not static, compact, not only of thought, but of passion and will; "faith is self-active." By virtue of the correspondence with the Creator which it establishes it is itself creative. In a sense and from the manward (though not the Godward) angle it creates the God in whom it trusts and a co-ordination of contraries which God alone can cause. "Faith is the anticipation of the eternal which holds the factors together, the cleavages of existence." And it is only in faith that God exists for man at all. For "God does not *exist*, he only is . . . he can only exist in faith" (J. 605).

Faith is thus the medium in which alone a God of pure being can be known in our life of becoming, of existential experience. But such an incarnation of the divine in human apprehension is something which, though he may and must go out to meet the miracle by an act of will, man cannot cause. Therefore "faith itself is a miracle." It is not gained; it is given. Miguel de Unanumo is thus echoing and amplifying the thought of Kierkegaard (whose leadership he acknowledged) concerning faith when he writes that "faith in its essence is simply a matter of will" and that "faith in God is born of love for God" and is "a movement of the soul towards a practical truth, towards a person, towards something that makes us not only comprehend life, but makes us live" (*The Tragic Sense of Life*, pp. 114, 150, 191).

It is, indeed, as an act of love, and so of passion, that Kierkegaard conceived Christian faith, and it is only by the analogy of love that it can really be interpreted. He turns, like Pascal, from the aridities of scholastic theology to the *connaissances du cœur*, the intuitions of the heart and an intelligence *vive et lumineuse*, live and luminous, by return to its existential sources. This ardent, loving and living faith in a loving and living God is, in fact, the faith of love – that new life of utter trust and new-born understanding which every lover knows, a faith which lives and feeds on love, "a love which talks with better knowledge and knowledge with dearer love" (*Measure for Measure*). Such a love-faith and love-knowledge are ever, for the uninitiated, a faith in 'the absurd' and the paradoxical; it is a faith which, in some sense, seems to create its own object and its own co-ordination of previous contraries.

Such a love-faith is therefore a living faith which must, of its own nature, reproduce itself in a life which flowers only in love and life, which harvests its own comprehension of that which, for the loveless, seems absurd as it loves and lives, which learns its doctrine not by abstract thinking, but in the doing of love's will. It is a secret wisdom common to all the wise in Christ (and in love). Kierkegaard is only repeating in the idiom of his own age a knowledge of the real nature of Christian faith which practising Christians such as Wyclif, with his "Love and good life are needful to right belief", have proclaimed throughout the Christian centuries. Therefore, for Kierkegaard, faith passes beyond the ethical to the religious category; "the opposite of sin is not virtue . . . the opposite of sin is faith" (S.D. p. 132).

It is a dynamic and existential conception of the nature of faith which seems indeed to harmonize with that of the Bible where we are told not to know, but to love God, and faith is always envisaged as a creative force. "If ye will not have faith ye shall not have staith" – so runs an early English version of the saying from Isaiah (vii. 9); faith is that which lays the foundations of life. "The just shall live by his faith", says Habakkuk in a prophecy echoed by St. Paul; faith is the fountain, not merely of thought, but of life. In the gospels and the words of Jesus faith is always the concomitant of power, and the writer of the Epistle to the Hebrews chronicles the fruits of faith as not theories, theologies or dogmatic rectitude, but 'mighty works.' Like the biblical conception of the Memra-Word of God, faith, in the Bible, as for Kierkegaard, is "a concrete event, a personal communication . . . bringing salvation" (*Communion in the Messiah*, by Lev Gillet, pp. 111–113). Kierkegaard's doctrine of faith was thus no innovation but rather the reassertion of an ancient biblical truth forgotten by an age gone a-whoring after humanism.

For Kierkegaard, therefore, Christian faith not only points to but is Christian living. It is a 'new life', born from the death of the autonomous natural self; it is a "dying into life." It is therefore, like the paradox of the Incarnation, an 'offence' for unregenerate reason. Offence and faith are, indeed, almost equated for him. "So inseparable from faith is the possibility of offence that if the God-man were not the possibility of offence, he could not be the object of faith" (T.C. p. 143). "This is the very first utterance of the New Testament", he declares, "that Christianity, and the fact that one is truly a Christian, must be in the highest degree an 'offence' to the natural man . . . being the thing that defines man as spirit, [it] must so appear to everyone

who has not by 'dying from' been reborn as 'spirit' . . .
As soon as Christianity is again presented in its true form,
then the true judgement will come out: 'It is treason
against humanity'" (S.E. 154-5). "The possibility of
offence is the dialectical factor in everything Christian"; it
is that which constitutes its constant challenge to the
complacent humanism of the human heart and mind.

That offence arises from the "infinite qualitative difference" between God and man; "that there is an infinite
difference of quality between God and man is the possibility of offence which cannot be taken away" (S.D.
p. 209). The offence of faith is thus, for Kierkegaard, rooted
in transcendence, and it seems to be from this intransigent
insistence upon the transcendence of God that the 'wholly
other' doctrine of Barthianism is derived. But in Kierkegaard this 'offensive' doctrine of divine transcendence is, as
has been seen, coupled with an equal insistence upon 'inwardness'. This transcendent Deity, the 'kingdom of
heaven', are not only other than and above man, they are
also 'within'.

Kierkegaard is thus affirming not transcendence only,
but a transcendence in immanence, a Christ and a 'kingdom
of heaven' which, as Blake also affirmed, are both above and
within. Here too the trend of modern thought follows his
lead. The 'personalism' of Berdyaev and many others to-
day is based upon the same paradoxical conception of the
nature of reality, man and faith. "There is a divine element
in man", writes Berdyaev, "Man is a being who surmounts
and transcends himself. . . . Personality is confronted by the
transcendent and in realizing itself it transcends" (*Slavery
and Freedom*, pp. 30, 45, 52). But Kierkegaard was chiefly
concerned to counteract the overweening immanentism of
contemporary thought; it has remained for descendants
from his doctrine to develop the full and balancing implications of his creed of Christian inwardness.

If such a faith was an 'offense' it was also a martyrdom. For Kierkegaard, as for most intellectuals, it was primarily a martyrdom of mind. The renewing of the "spirit of the mind", like the whole process of spiritual rebirth, was, for him as for William Law, not "a thing done, but . . . a thing continually doing" (*Mystical Writings*, p. 22). "The martyrdom of faith (crucifixion of the understanding) is not a martyrdom of the instant but precisely the martyrdom of endurance" (U.P. p. 496). For the impulses of the natural mind, like those of the will, constantly reassert themselves, and by the Christian must as constantly be mortified and reversed. Homocentric humanism dies hard in the modern mind in the texture of which its habit has been long and deeply ingrained.

For Kierkegaard Christianity implied also an external martyrdom which, in his own fashion, he endured. His journals suggest that he expected even a physical martyrdom as the reward of his Christian "contumacy" and attack upon official Christianity. But the traditional pattern of martyrdom did not fall to his lot, except in so far as a frail constitution impaired, and a perhaps premature death caused by the prodigious labours which his faith exacted and the infirmity to which he frequently refers as his "thorn in the flesh" are concerned. He endured what he has called the "martyrdom of laughter" in his controversy with *The Corsair*. "I have been made a laughing-stock", he writes in 1849, "that is the martyrdom I have suffered . . . I am the martyr of laughter; for not everyone who suffers being laughed at, even though for an idea, is strictly speaking a martyr of laughter . . . But I am the martyr of laughter . . . I myself could have commanded laughter on an unequalled scale . . . and so have become just what the age desired . . . And quite rightly I had to command laughter to turn on me" (J. 880). In other words, he had deliberately become "a fool for Christ's sake"; for a man of his natural pride, wit

and fastidious sensibility it was a persecution not easily to
be endured.

In his renunciation of Regina, whatever the merits or
demerits of the course which he felt constrained to adopt,
he had also incurred a martyrdom of feeling far more acute
and enduring. It is impossible to read his story without
realizing that, in making that sacrifice, he was losing his
natural life, his 'first immediacy', and inviting a slow
martyrdom of that life which lasted to the end of his days.
It was more than the sacrifice of love; it was the sacrifice of
life. For all his natural human life had come to a burning
point in that passion. He at least was convinced that its renunciation and the martyrdom of his manhood which it
entailed were the inexorable requirements for him of his
Christian faith.

But his real martyrdom and the real meaning of martyrdom for him was, like his faith, a matter of 'inwardness'.
Such inwardness involved a profound inward suffering of
spirit in a continual and increasing awareness laying open
ever deeper levels of consciousness to the searching and con-
suming fire of the Spirit. He who essays to search his heart
and hidden motives invites an end to his equanimity, a
stripping of self to the buff, a despair and dereliction, an
agony of self-dissolution which those "whose sails were
never to the tempest given" can neither know nor guess.
So "secret", as J. H. Mozley exclaimed, "is the system of
temptation". Here is the real inward martyrdom of man.
Therefore, as Kierkegaard declared, "Christianity is the
deepest wound which can be inflicted upon a man" (L.
p. 535).

That inward martyrdom and mortification is also a sacrifice, self-incurred, in which the self is both the sacrificial
priest and the victim after the pattern of his Lord. "According to the New Testament", he writes, "to be a Christian
properly means . . . to be sacrificed." That wound and

sacrifice are incurred, he affirmed, in the very choice of despair and selfhood and the aloneness which such a selfhood involves. It is a sacrifice which the Christian is called not only to endure but passionately to desire. "When one is able to endure the isolation involved in being a single individual . . . alone in the endless world and the endless world of men . . . alone before the face of God – then . . . he must say: O my God, now I have but one wish, one prayer, one desire, one passion, that I may experience suffering, become hated, persecuted, mocked, spit upon, put to death . . . Behold, this is the passion for martyrdom" (L. p. 542). It is in that following of Christ along the way of self-sacrifice, that sanctification by his blood, that the difference (obscure to the sceptic) between masochism and martyrdom consists.

Such a voluntary self-martyrdom, such a devastating solitude and sincerity of spirit before God are, Kierkegaard affirmed, "the bold adventure which is required of us." Such sayings, emphazing the solitude of the Christian 'venture' of spirit with which his writings are starred, have earned for him, from more gregarious and scornful critics, the stricture of 'solitudinarianism' – a wilful self-seclusion from the society of men, the saints and the community of the Church. That such an aloneness "before the face of God" was a way deliberately chosen his self-revelations amply attest. He certainly conceived such an aloneness to be incumbent upon the real follower of Christ and particularly incumbent, in his particular situation, upon him. This was the martyrdom to which he believed himself called. "What the age needs", he said, "is not a genius . . . but a martyr"; "Denmark has need of a dead man" – that is, of one really 'dead to the world'." For he believed himself to be 'the exception', a man chosen by God to stand out from the misled crowd of so-called Christians and sound the "cry of alarm." Such a role demanded isolation if it were to be faithfully fulfilled. "If the crowd is the evil", so he reasoned, "if chaos is what threatens us, there is salvation only in one thing, in becoming a single individual in the thought of 'that individual' as an essential category" (P.V. p. 61). The chaos, of which he beheld the threat as of a "cloud the size of a man's hand", has come upon us and the worth and freedom of the individual are assailed on every hand. That Kierkegaard, in that he thus foresaw the shape of "things to come", was an 'exception' now needs no argument.

Such a solitude of spirit is indeed the lot of all 'exceptions', of all who are called to stem the mass-movements of a deluded majority. It is the aloneness which every leader incurs – such an aloneness as that which Bernard Shaw voices in his *St. Joan*: "France is alone; and God is alone; and what is my loneliness before the loneliness of my country and my God? I see now that the loneliness of God is his strength . . . it is better to be alone with God." So it was that Kierkegaard conceived of the essential solitude of spirit of a real Christianity. Nevertheless – it seems a paradox as existentially true of spiritual as of philosophic solitude – he who can attain and endure such a solitude finds a community with life and man in God, the All, which can be found by no way less 'strait' and can, in the end, affirm that he is "never less alone than when alone." Christian solitude is the 'strait way' to true Christian community.

But his conviction that loneliness was the lot of real Christians was not limited to his own particular destiny, though that destiny made it more acute for him; it was, he believed, the "flight of the alone to the Alone" (in the phrase of Plotinus) to which a true Christian inwardness inevitably called – the way of the Cross. For he was convinced that "the individual is the category of spirit, of spiritual awakening." And "as a single individual" the

Christian "is alone, alone in the whole world, alone before
God." Therefore a Christianity of inwardness and the
spirit required a realization and rebirth of individual selfhood which, in itself, inevitably means an inward martyrdom of the natural, the 'old man.'

Solitude and the life of spirit were thus for him a single
way and life. It seems an inescapable conclusion. It is only
when a man communes in solitude with his own heart and
God that he can enter the dimension of spirit at all, and it is
only when he can dare to be alone that he can hear the
word of God or discern "truth in the inward parts". And it
is upon this "naked intent", this personal 'appropriation'
of the word of God in the Bible, that Kierkegaard bases his
belief. Here too the affinity of his faith to that of Pascal is
clear. For Pascal heard, he declares, the voice of Christ
assuring him that "I am present with thee by my word in
Scripture"; it was the persuasion of Kierkegaard also. But
he can only know that presence and that Voice in stillness
and solitude of spirit. "He who is not alone with God's
Word", he wrote, "is not reading God's Word." "I have
never seen anyone", he adds, "whom I could venture to
believe that he had sincerity and courage enough to be so
completely alone with God's Word that absolutely no illusion surreptitiously intruded" (S.E. p. 55). Thus for Kierkegaard such a solitude of spirit, like inwardness and faith, is
also a process of becoming in our life; we cannot here and
now fully attain, we move towards, that final loneliness
with 'God only', following in the footsteps of the Lord.

Thus solitude with 'God only' is for Kierkegaard part of
the daring, the risk, the 'leap' which he believes an essential
Christianity to be. It is the essential solitude of every soul
which dares to become aware of itself and its destiny. There
is ample evidence that the choice of such a solitude was,
for him, due to no morose self-centredness. In his undergraduate days he had been the most "clubbable" of men, the

centre of a wide circle of friends, and throughout his life
it was his practice and pleasure to mix daily with the
Copenhagen crowds. His solitude was inward and one, not
of natural predilection, but of inner compulsion; it was, for
him, the 'strait way' of Christ. It was a solitude replete, not
only with that "joy of the Lord" which came to him at
last, but with "pale, bloodless, midnight shapes", with
"dread and trembling", a solitude in which, as Gerard
Manley Hopkins (in so many ways his peer in the life of the
spirit) was to write long afterwards –

"We hear our hearts grate on themselves . . .
. . . this tormenting mind
With this tormenting mind tormenting yet."

It is in this solitude, this "dark night of the spirit", that
Kierkegaard finds the real and inward martyrdom of the
Christian man. It is of such an inward martyrdom that he
declares that "the nervous system of Christianity meets in
the reality of martyrdom." We are here again in the presence of something which only the paradoxical logic of
love can interpret. For here are the solitude and passion
of the lover – a solitude which is delight and dereliction
at the same time, a passion which is both joy and pain.
This was for him the price of love and the "pearl of great
price" of ultimate, inward reality for which he gave "all
that he had." It is a secret obscure for the casuist but open
for the mystic.

The Christian way thus meant for Kierkegaard a passionate following along the way of the Cross to an inward
world of spirit, stripped and stark as some high glacier up-
land from which the life-giving waters flow down to the
life of men. It is the following, not the formula, that matters. "The proof of Christianity really consists in the
'following'," he says (S.E. p. 88). "There is only one way
of being a Christian – to be a disciple" (S.E. p. 215). "Save

us", he prayed, "from the error of wishing to admire Thee instead of being willing to follow Thee" (T.C. p. 227). And discipleship requires renunciation. But renunciation is the lover's own reward. He speaks of "the delight of renunciation" as "simply a lover's understanding with God . . . it was as though God had whispered the secret to me. Renunciation is a higher relation to God, it is really a love-relationship: and for me at least an enchantment was spread over renunciation" (J. 1279). It is the very language of love.

In his conception of the way and the life of a real and existential Christianity, the thought, feeling and language of Kierkegaard are thus always and, as he moves towards spiritual maturity, increasingly those of a lover. There is the heart of his mystery, of his inwardness, his agonies, his solitude, his dyings, his martyrdom, his emphasis upon now the severity and now the gentleness of Christianity. It is a note which sounds more and more clearly through his later writings, such as *Training in Christianity*, *Discourses at the Communion on Fridays*, *For Self-Examination* and *Judge for Yourself*. These books are devoted not to the theory but to the practice of the Christian life – the mystery, following and discipline of love.

Thus the lover's life, he writes in the preface to his Discourses, "is my very life, the content of my life for me, its fullness, its happiness, its peace and contentment" (S.E. p. 11). "Love's judgement is the severest judgement", he writes. "Learn to fear, not the severity of justice, but the gentleness of love". "Love pierces far more deeply into life, to the very issues of life, than does justice"; "love, whose condemnation is (oh, frightful condemnation!) 'Thy sins are forgiven thee' "; "of one fault we are all guilty more or less: of loving too little" (S.E. 12, 13). Just so St.-John-of-the-Cross declared "in the evening they will examine thee in love." And it is with the eyes of love that the word of God can alone rightly be read. "Think of a lover", he says, "who has now received a letter from his beloved – as precious as this letter is to the lover, just so precious to thee, I assume, is God's Word" (S.E. p. 51). These are intimations and insights with which all existential experience of the life of love is familiar; they are only comprehensible in that light.

It is thus in love that he finds "nature's profoundest myth" and in religion "the highest love." "This God-relationship of mine," he declares, "is the 'happy love' in a life which has always been troubled and unhappy" (P.V. p. 64). For a certain school of psychological criticism a spiritual love thus derived from a frustrated physical love is readily written off as "compensatory illusion." But in this case, such a conclusion seems to incur the criticism of being itself unrealistic. For reality does not arise from unreality, and it is impossible to study Kierkegaard's life and work without prejudice and fail to realize the ardent reality of this love-relationship to which, in the end, Christianity resolved itself for him. It was inescapably and ruthlessly real and was itself the crown and consummation of the exacting existential realism which was his first principle.

Moreover Kierkegaard's interpretation of the Christian mystery as essentially a 'love-story' penetrates far beyond the romance of "love's young dream" to the fulfilment and realism of marital love and fidelity. In view of his own renunciation of the state of marriage, his estimation of the real meaning and worth of marriage for the life of religion is a surprising token of his genius and charity. A bitter cynicism or a blindness to the true significance of marriage might have been expected; in fact we find precisely the reverse.

He was fully conscious of the apparent and difficult Christian dilemma which sexual and marital life present, and of the merits and demerits of the classic solution of that dilemma by the medieval church of celibacy for saints but marriage for sinners as a remedy against being "burned", and of the apparent impossibility of reconciling the life of generation with that of regeneration. "The unmarried man," he wrote, "can make greater ventures in the life of spirit than the married man, he can stake everything" (St. p. 244). And "it is quite certain and true that Christianity is suspicious of marriage" (T.C. p. 119).

Nevertheless it was in marriage that he perceived the true completion of the Christian life and in a comprehension to which only the well married can attain the true meaning of its mystery. A paper on marriage written late in his life contains some of the most penetrating of his utterances on this matter. "Every other sort of acquaintance with life," he declares, "is superficial in comparison with that acquired by the married man, for he and he alone has thoroughly fathomed the depths of life." "Only a married man is a genuine man." It is, he affirms, in this wisdom of marriage that the Christian excels the pagan comprehension of life; "in paganism there is a God for love but none for marriage; in Christianity there is . . . a God for marriage and none for love." Like Christianity as he conceives it, marriage is "the synthesis of love and resolution", for marriage, like faith, demands decision. Marriage is "the beauteous mid-point and centre of human existence." It is more; in marriage he perceives what he means by the 'instant'. "Marriage is the fullness of time." And marriage gives access to the deepest reality possible for mortality; a mother "belongs completely to reality."

Kierkegaard never explores the full spiritual significance of these insights into the crucial importance for Christianity of the fact and concept of marriage, or the nature, in that context, of the true ultimate Christian resolution of the generation: regeneration dilemma. It may be surmised that he felt that his own experience, frustrated of that fulfilment,

G

disqualified him for such a task. But there can be no doubt that he saw in marriage the type in time of the true Christian consummation and in a psychological and spiritual marriage the supreme co-ordination of our existential contraries.

In that insight he is at one with a great crowd of Christian witness. No realistic reading of the Bible can evade the realization that the marriage-motif is dominant throughout that book. A continuing Christian tradition, of which St. Bernard, St.-John-of-the-Cross, Ruysbroek and St. Teresa are salient exponents, has found in the *Song of Songs* the perpetual prototype and symbol of the 'spiritual marriage'. Origen wrote of the "intercourse of the Word, the Bridegroom, with the soul, the bride" and St. Augustine that "the soul hath in God her lawful husband." "I cannot contain myself for joy that the Divine Majesty disdains not to . . . enter into marriage with a soul still in exile", wrote St. Bernard (*Canticle* lii. 2). For Ruysbroek the "Bridegroom is Christ, and human nature is the bride" and "nothing is more joyful to the lover of God, than to feel that he belongs wholly to his Beloved" (*Adornment of the Spiritual Marriage*). St.-John-of-the-Cross speaks of "the consummation of this most happy state of marriage with Him" (*Spiritual Canticles*) and sees in "this flame of love . . . the Spirit of the Spouse – that is, the Holy Spirit" (*The Living Flame of Love*). In our own age Coventry Patmore wrote that "God has declared to us his mystic rapture in his marriage with humanity . . . This is the burning heart of the universe" (*Aphorisms and Extracts*). Comparison of such sayings with those of Kierkegaard leaves little room for doubt that for him also in this concept and fact of the 'spiritual marriage' was the "burning heart" of his faith, and that in this respect also he was rather rediscovering a repressed Christian realism than departing from the great tradition.

Here too, though concerning this aspect of Christianity

he rather points than explores, Kierkegaard's existential Christianity speaks to a real and deep need of the consciousness of our own as of his day. For, as with regard to the subconscious, so with regard to sexuality, established and 'safe' Christianity has signally failed to confront the real issues or to proclaim the real remedy for psychological and sexual ills which the Christian treasury of truth contains. It is only, as Kierkegaard saw and insisted, upon the plane of spirit that these inner and corroding conflicts of consciousness can be co-ordinated and to that co-ordination the Church, so he believed, holds, but, from failure of realism and nerve, hides the key. "Ye have taken away the key of knowledge: ye entered not in yourselves, and them that were entering in ye hindered". Such was, in effect, Kierkegaard's indictment of the Christianity of his day. It remains his challenge to our own.

The tortured division of consciousness, dialectic of thought and life, despair, gloom and rigour which characterize Kierkegaard's first arduous wrestlings with religious reality thus led him at last to the gentleness and simplicity of a Christianity which is essentially a 'love-story'. It is perhaps in part due to the fact that the majority of his critics have not themselves passed beyond that grim first phase, that our world wanders yet in its own 'waste land', that the prevailing conception of the man and his thought is one of conflict, despair and austerity and the "love, joy, peace", the "simplicity which is in Christ" to which he won and in which his real gospel for our condition is to be found, are normally neglected. His initial desperate struggle was as grim as that which racks us to-day; but the faith which overcame that world of woe was as gay, as radiant and as simple as that of the first followers of Christ.

For Kierkegaard the simplicity and gentleness of Christ are not prizes easily won; they are the hard and high reward of strenuous spiritual endeavour and discipline. From the

first he had recognized that simplicity as the hallmark of
the true wisdom; it was as a "simple wise man" that he
venerated Socrates. But for him "the movement is not from
the simple to the interesting but from the interesting to the
simple." That movement is itself the "thing of becoming a
Christian." "To become again a child . . . to *will* to . . .
retain youth's spontaneous enthusiasm with its spontaneity
unabated, to *will* to reacquire it by valiant effort . . . that is
the task" (T.C. p. 190). "In a Christian sense simplicity is
not the point of departure from which one goes on to become interesting, witty, profound, poet, philosopher, etc.
No, the very contrary. *Here* one begins (with the interesting, etc.) and becomes simpler and simpler, *attaining*
simplicity" (P.V. p. 148). Such, at all events, was his own
course, and here too, it would seem that he has a special
leading for intellectuals "bowed with the infirmity" of a
complex and disintegrated consciousness, unable to be
"made straight" in simplicity and so glorify God. That
Kierkegaard himself attained to a large measure of the
loving simplicity which he had seen afar off and sought his
latest utterances testify.

His attitude towards the contrasted severity and gentleness of Christianity is the same. He believed that Christianity
had become corrupt with a false gentleness – the sickly
gentleness of the Victorian "gentle Jesus, meek and mild".
"Christianity was abolished in Christendom", he wrote,
"by gentleness . . . there is only one salvation; severity"
(T.C. p. 222). But he knew that severity and gentleness or
'leniency' were as dark and light, night and day, of the
single orb of the paradoxical Christian reality. "In my presentation", he says, "severity is the dialectical moment in
Christianity, but leniency is just as strongly represented . . .
If I had understood only its frightful severity—then I should
have kept silent . . . For a merely negative result . . . one
must not communicate" (L. p. 448). He never wavers in

his certainty of the gentleness of God and of a real Christianity, and as his life moves towards its close, and especially after his second conversion in 1848, his assertion of that verity grows more constant and emphatic. In 1843 he had written, "God is certainly love, but not love to sinners" (J. 442), but in 1849, "God is gentle. That I have always understood. My own life shows me that" (J. 1005). And in 1850, "This is all I have known for certain, that God is love . . . His love is a spring which never runs dry" (J. 1102). And at last, in 1853, in a rapturous repetitive refrain, "how endlessly thou art loved" (J. p. 563). To such a childlike simplicity, love and peace had his conflict and complexity come.

For Kierkegaard the pith of the Christian way and life was thus a dynamic faith in a divine Spirit transcendent in our immanence, belief which is also being, a Christian realism of inwardness and reborn individuality ever deepening to the essence, to an inward martyrdom of 'dying into life', to a personal 'appropriation' of the word of God, to a conception of real Christianity as a 'love-story' and so to its consummation as a 'spiritual marriage.' It was thus to a Christianity of the spirit that his existential conceiving came.

But, the inner conflict resolved, an outward conflict came upon him. For this was a faith which inevitably involved conflict with an established Christianity confined, so he believed, to the 'letter' of the Christian law. His conception of a Christianity of the spirit, of the nature of the Church and the apostasy of the churches are the sequel to the personal faith which has been considered.

6

Religion A and Religion B

IN the course of his religious experience Kierkegaard had come to discriminate between what he termed "religious-ness A and B". By 'religiousness A' he intended, in general, a religion of immanence and the 'first immediacy' of nature; and by 'religiousness B' a religion of transcendence, the 'second immediacy' and grace. The conflict between these two forms of 'religiousness' in his own case had been acute. It was inevitable, therefore, that when his own faith and conception of a real Christianity had crystallized as 'religiousness B', his inner conflict should become extern-alized in an attack upon the 'religiousness A' which, so he believed, the established church in Denmark was purveying to the "hungry sheep" of its flock as Christianity.

He was, in fact, assaulting that which, 'writ large' in popular and officially-sponsored 'religiosity', he had fought and overcome in his own soul. Until the second spiritual crisis of 1848 – when he heard the call to action, believed himself to be at last made whole in spirit and wrote, "I must speak" – the war with religion A had been con-fined to his own consciousness. After that date it became increasingly a war waged against the same foe in the out-ward world. It was, in little and in anticipation, the conflict with which all Christendom is confronted to-day.

It was no merely theoretic distinction which he drew between these forms of religion, but one based upon personal and poignant experience – an arduous and perilous migration from an old to a new world of the spirit. He had himself passed from the one world of consciousness to the other. It had meant for him no smooth passage, no continu-ity from one way of life and form of thought and faith to another more mature and profound, but a "leap in the dark", a catastrophic dying to the "first immediacy" of nature and an anguished rebirth "from above" into the "second immediacy" of grace, of the 'new man'. He knew well the lure of the religiousness which, by every shift and sleight of self-justification, seeks to evade that catastrophic 'instant' of judgement and 'dying into life' in which religion A is reborn into religion B and, in a counterfeit Christianity, to escape the perils and ardours of that new life of spirit and real Christianity which, for him, constituted religion B. He knew too, in his own soul, the unceasing trend and temptation to "revert to an earlier condition", to relapse into the comfortable religiosity of "religiousness A."

For Kierkegaard these two contrasted forms of religion are divided and distinguished, first, by the historical fact of the Incarnation and, second, by the realization of sin (in distinction from the sense of guilt) caused by confrontation with that fact. It is the coming of the God-man into our actual human existence and history which sets a wall of fire between these two forms of faith. "In religiousness A", he writes, "there is no historical starting-point"; the eternal, the God-man, has not entered into history but only into imagination. Religion A is therefore a religion of recollection and immanence. "In time the individual recollects that he is eternal" (U.P. p. 508). And, since for such religion God and eternity dwell, not in his existence, but in his imagination, it is only in man's own imagination and will that he can seek salvation by "the individual's own pathetic transformation of existence" (U.P. p. 515). Since such a God is not a person, but an idea, and sin can only exist in relation to a person, such religion knows guilt but does not yet know sin. Such a religion is thus, in Dr. Lowrie's words, "simply a heartfelt expression of a sense of God, or of the numinous" (L. p. 325).

Religion A – commonly called Christianity in Christendom – is thus a religion between which and other 'high religions' there is no essential difference. Modern attempts to blend a basic wisdom common to all the wise among men and a 'basic Christianity' in a 'Federation of Faiths' are thus of this order. For Kierkegaard this is genuine religion – 'religiousness A'' – and it may be magnificent; but it is not Christianity.

Into religion B, however, to which for Kierkegaard real Christianity is confined, the Incarnation, the God-man, Christ has come. God has become man, eternity has entered time, being has invaded becoming and essence existence at a precise historical time and place. This is the crucial paradox and 'offence' which differentiates religion B absolutely from religion A and fixes a great gulf between them. Therefore the individual for whom the Incarnation has become fact and no longer fancy is immediately confronted with God and eternity, not in idea only, but in his actual existence. "As the eternal came into the world at a moment of time, the existing individual does not in the course of time come into relation with the eternal and think about it (this is A), but *in time* it comes into relation with the eternal *in time*" (U.P. p. 506). In that relation and context the individual is reborn into the dimension of spirit and eternal life. "The individual who was eternal now becomes such, and so does not recollect what he is but becomes what he was not" (U.P. p. 508). In fact, in Kierkegaard's terminology, he has entered the category of 'repetition'; "what has been now becomes."

But this new life of selfhood, spirit and eternity is not an abstraction from but concrete (growing with) within existential reality. It is in our actual existence, not in some 'other world', that this new and eternal life is born and becomes. Since the eternal has entered time, therefore, for religion B, "only in existing do I become eternal." More-

over, here, in this direct relation of eternity with time, God
with man, in our existence, guilt becomes sin. For while
man in religion A knows guilt towards an 'Unknown
God', sin is offence against a person and, in the Incarnation
and religion B, the self is confronted with the person of the
God-man, Jesus Christ.

Religion B is thus, by virtue of the Incarnation, a faith
peculiar to Christianity; it is therefore unique among religions, 'high' or 'low', and in this crucial respect 'wholly
other' than they as a religion of and in history. The possibility of 'federation' with other faiths and forms of religion A is therefore excluded, for the federation (though not
the marriage) of God and man, eternity and time, spirit and
flesh is no more than fantasy.

Christianity is thus the only example of religion B. Its
real power and challenge consist in that uniqueness. Again
to quote Dr. Lowrie, it is a religion of "eternity *in* time,
challenging time, conflicting with time, and looking forward eschatalogically to the termination of time" (L.
pp. 323–4). It is "essentially paradoxical" – no 'faint trust' in
some 'larger hope', no mere numinous memory or apprehension of God and eternity, no human attempt to transform
existence, but "the paradoxical transformation of existence
by faith through relation to an historic fact" (U.P. p. 515).
Here alone sin becomes a reality and such a "sin-con-
sciousness is the breach with immanence" – and with religion A. And not only is existence transformed by this faith,
the self which thus confronts Christ in existence is reborn,
not from within by its own effort, but 'from above.'

Kierkegaard is no bigot; he does not suggest that
these two forms of religion are absolute and irreconcilable
contraries; he seems to conceive rather of the transcendent
"paradoxical religiousness B of the second immediacy" as
proceeding, reborn, from the "religiousness A" of immanence and the 'first immediacy.' And, for him, with his

insistence upon the 'inwardness' of real religion, the transcendence of religion B is a transcendence in immanence; it
is within existence that this transcendent kingdom of the
God-man and eternal life comes to pass.

But he insists upon the absolute distinction between them,
upon the fact that, by virtue of the paradox of the Incarnation, properly speaking real Christianity is confined to
religion B and upon the catastrophic (not continuous or
evolutionary) character of the 'instant' in which A is transfigured, reborn into B. His primary quarrel is with an
aesthetic, speculative, erotic travesty of real religion
(whether A or B), which eludes any real confrontation with
the 'offence' and judgement of the Word, the God-man,
and abstracts religion from reality; his secondary quarrel is
with a 'religiousness A' which, though aware of the "infinite qualitative difference" between the two, masquerades
as 'religiousness B', as real Christianity, from cowardice,
complacency or love of ease. It is upon both these counts
that he indicts the established, official Christianity of his day.

Religion B, which he thus identifies with a real Christianity, is not only unique among religions by virtue of the
Incarnation; it is also the only real religion 'after the spirit.'
For, in religion B, the concept of spirit is something quite
distinct from that which the term connotes for religion A.
For the former it is both transcendent and concrete, for the
latter it is abstract from and immanent within man and his
world; for the one spirit is a Person, for the other it is a
ghost, a fairy-tale or a dream. Spirit, he declared, "is the
negation of direct immediacy"; it is that which mortifies
the life of nature and, in that dying and self-losing, regener-
ates it to eternal life. "Into this night of hopelessness – it is in
fact death that we are describing – comes then the life-giving
Spirit and brings hope – the hope of eternity" (S.E. p. 101).
On the other hand the religion A of 'direct immediacy' is a
religion of and in time and, according to Kierkegaard, "the

temporal never is and never will be the element of spirit"
(P.V. p. 82).

For Kierkegaard, moreover, spirit is no phantom, no
"visitor within this creature", as for Neo-Platonism and
non-Christian mysticism. Man, he says, "is a synthesis of the
soulish and the bodily. But the synthesis is unthinkable
where the two are not united by a third. This third is spirit".
He equates spirit with the 'self', the reborn individual;
"spirit is the self." Spirit is both that which begets the self
upon the natural consciousness or soul of man in a fusion
or marriage of the "synthesis of the infinite and the finite,
of the temporal and the eternal, of freedom and necessity"
which, by nature, man is, and the being of the reborn self
which is begotten from that marriage. Spirit is thus that
which begets the real and eternal self and, in that new birth
'from above' (which is also 'within'), transfigures soul into
spirit. But, in that transfiguration, man and matter, though
thus transfigured into spirit-being and eternalized, remain
man and matter. The life of spirit is that of humanity and
the world redeemed, transfigured, not annulled, and that
redemption is only possible by virtue of the paradox of the
Incarnation and for religion B. The life of grace and spirit
is thus, not abstract from the life of nature, but concrete,
growing within it – that life fulfilled. Therefore real
Christianity (confined, for Kierkegaard, to religion B) is
life 'after' (or in the power of) spirit, while religion A is
life 'after the flesh'.

Kierkegaard's antithesis is thus substantially the same as
that of St. Paul in the Epistle to the Romans. For him as
for Paul, that deep difference is a matter of mortal urgency.
For he, like Paul, believed passionately that "if [we] live
after the flesh [that is, a life limited to the 'first immediacy']
[we] shall die" (as all flesh must die), but that if "we
mortify the motives (or impulses) of the flesh (in inwardness, aloneness with God and the life of spirit), in the power

of the Spirit, we shall live – the life of the 'second immediacy' which is eternal life. It is thus an issue of eternal
life or death. Therefore he dare not compromise or fail to
"speak with boldness" what he has seen and heard. Therefore he was constrained to assail that which he most
cherished – his own Mother Church. It was with the anguished austerity with which Hamlet was impelled by his
own integrity to upbraid his mother Gertrude for her
betrayal of his father that he did so. Just so, it seeemd to
Kierkegaard, his Mother Church of Denmark had betrayed
God the Father with the treacherous Claudius of a counterfeit Christianity.

But his astringent criticism of his church – *a* church –
was no denial of the claims of *the* Church. From first to last
Kierkegaard was, indeed, a devoted church-man, a faithful
attendant at the services, and especially at the communions,
of the Church. It was only at the last and as a final gesture
of protest, that he refused the communion from a clergyman
of the established church. He not only attended, he also
assisted the services of the church as his *Religious Discourses*
attest. And, throughout his life, he contemplated ordination.
That he never actually took that step was due rather to an
exalted conception of the office of priesthood, an acute contrition for past sin and sense of his own inadequacy for so
high and holy a function and to an integrity which refused
the material security which a 'living' offered, than to
any depreciation of its importance.

He held, indeed, at all events at one time, an extreme
'Catholic' view of the character of the priesthood. A priest,
he wrote, "is essentially what he is through ordination and
ordination is a . . . paradoxical transformation in time, by
which he becomes, in time, something else . . . ordination
constitutes a *character indelebilis*" (U.P. p. 244). There seems
some reason to suppose that he afterwards modified this
extreme view of the priestly 'character', but none that he

reduced his veneration for the office. He held a view no less 'high' of the authority of the priesthood. "A priest *must* use authority, he *must* say to men: *You shall*; he must do that even though they put him to death" (J. 716). But he finds that "alas, a true priest is even more rare than a true poet" (S.D. p 166).

His own vocation to the priesthood never ceased to sound in his ears. His sacrifice of that deep desire was as bitter – and, indeed, of the same nature – as his sacrifice of his hopes of marriage; in each case it was dictated by his overmastering sense of mission and of unfitness. In 1846 he writes, "The wish to be a priest in the country has always attracted me." In 1847 financial stringency suggested a 'living' as a means of subsistence and security and in 1848 he writes, "Now by God's help I shall become myself . . . and then I will become a priest." But his congenital melancholy, an exaggerated remorse for the sins of his youth and fear of causing scandal to the Church deterred him, and he was not the man so to purchase material security. Moreover he seems to have felt that, if he were to fulfil what he believed to be his mission to sound a 'cry of alarm' and denounce what he believed to be the counterfeit Christianity of the established church, he must remain free and unfettered by professional loyalties.

It was not, therefore, from any underestimate of the cruciality of the Church for a real Christianity that he either refrained from taking holy orders himself or attacked the established church in Denmark. He was, indeed, a staunch Catholic in his attitude towards the "Holy, Catholic and Apostolic Church". Nevertheless, for 'churchianity' he had no sympathy; "the deification of the Church", he wrote, "is nothing but permanent rebellion against God" (L. p. 428). Protestantism, on the other hand, was for him not a faith or a church, but a 'corrective'. He wrote in 1838 that "there are on the whole few men who are able to bear the

Protestant view of life"; it was an attitude towards
Protestantism to which there is no good reason to suppose
that he did not adhere for the remainder of his life.

It was, in fact, on behalf of the Church of Christ that he
attacked the established church of Denmark. And by
establishment he meant more than the English technical
connotation of that term – a church come to terms with
secular society, become static rather than dynamic and conservative rather than creative, "settled on its lees", corrupted
by the enjoyment of place and the corruption of power. He
speaks of "the ungodly veneration of the established church
as divine", declares (with a strangely prophetic voice) that
"the deification of the established order is the seculariza-
tion of everything" and that "the established order desires
to be totalitarian" (T.C. p. 92). He saw this stigma of
'establishment' seducing the established church from her
chastity in Christ and her duty to 'God only'. "In established
Christianity", he wrote, "the natural man manages to have
his own way"; in other words, established Christianity
tends always to relapse from religion B to religion A, from
the second to the first 'immediacy', from a Christianity
'after the spirit' to a Christianity 'after the flesh.' Therefore,
for him, "established Christianity simply doesn't make
sense"; it is a contradiction in terms, and "established
Christendom . . . might be called the caricature of Christianity" (P.V. p. 77).

He saw the officials, the parsons, of such an established
Christianity as quite inevitably to some extent infected
by that corruption, however saintly in character they might
be. For they were, *ipso facto*, servants of the state rather than
of the spirit, professional men always liable to be concerned
rather with 'livings' and making a living than with the
gospel of eternal life, and officials caught up in the spirit-
quenching busy-ness of a bureaucratic machine. They were
doomed to become more or less hypocritical or (as the

Gospel word correctly implies) unrealist, alienated by temporal and worldly appearance from eternal realities.

His indictment, his declaration of 'Woe unto you' is as bold and severe as that of his Lord in what he conceived to be similar circumstances. For he stood for "religiousness absolute" (*i.e.*, religion B), of a different kind from that of the parsons. He speaks forth boldly, as he believes that he ought to speak. "What concerns the clergy is their livings ... official Christianity is both aesthetically and intellectually ludicrous and indecent, a scandal in the Christian sense" (L2. p. 246). He adds his irony to his invective. "Had St. Paul an official position? No. Had he any means of liveli-hood? No. Did he make a lot of money? No. Did he marry and have children? No. But in that case St. Paul was not a serious man" (J. 686). "Truly and seriously to give up all things is not a joke, like the parson's trash." "*Parson*: Thou shalt die unto the world.—The fee is one guinea."

But it is not so much simony as that with which simony adulterates Christianity which he assails most vehemently. For the parson, whose priesthood is his career and means of livelihood, is sorely tempted to accommodate his Christian-ity to worldly caution. "The modern clergyman is trained", he declares, "in the art of introducing Christianity in such a way that it signifies nothing" (J. 1305). "The so-called Church falsifies Christianity by watering it down" (J. 1358).

His mind was not lightly or swiftly made up on this matter. In 1849 he writes that he is "in the midst of the strain, of the struggle with ideas and questions of principle, whether, from the Christian point of view, there should be official Christian offices" (J. 928). In 1854 he thanks God that "he has prevented me from thoughtlessly becoming a parson in the sense that people here, nowadays, are parsons, which is to make a mockery of Christianity"; he believes it his duty to declare that "official divine worship is a mockery of God, and to take part in it a crime" (J. 1405). At the end of that year and a little less than a year before he died he at last launched a public attack upon the established church in the course of which he cried, "One thing I adjure thee for the sake of God in heaven and by all that is holy, shun the parsons" (L2. p. 252).

In this matter again his language must be read in the light of his conviction that it was his task to utter, not a cautious and considered judgement, but a 'corrective', and in a form which would gain a hearing. Nevertheless his challenge still stands, for the corruption of Christianity and Christendom which he foresaw and prophesied is to-day a fact which none can deny. But the corruption has spread since his day like a black-death; his challenge is now not merely to a church but to a world. He foresaw the judgement of Europe: it has come upon us. He proclaimed that in "religiousness absolute", religion B, a Christianity 'after the spirit' and therefore a radical Christian revolution, lay its sole salvation. His challenge remains; it seems not less but more relevant for our own day.

Kierkegaard's attitude towards our hollow civilization and Christianity has been allegorized by Franz Kafka in the opening to his novel *The Castle*: "It was late in the evening when K arrived. The village was deep in snow. The Castle hill was hidden, veiled in mist and darkness, nor was there even a glimmer of light to show that a castle was there. On the wooden bridge leading from the main road to the village K stood for a long time gazing into the illusory emptiness above him." So "late in the evening" of the first Christian age, Kierkegaard gazed into the "illusory emptiness" of Christendom and cried out with a loud voice that "Christianity no longer exists." His existential thinking denied its existence in our world; his faith stedfastly affirmed and re-affirmed its eternal and incorruptible essence, and its 'strait way'.

www.ingramcontent.com/pod-product-compliance
Lightning Source LLC
Chambersburg PA
CBHW071100090426
42737CB00013B/2403